Dark Cloud Country

Regeneration is Relationship!

PRAISE FOR

DARK CLOUD COUNTRY

"An impassioned celebration of life in all its complex wonderment."

—JAMES CANTON
Author of *The Oak Papers* and *Grounded*

"If you relish poetic writing, if you are in awe of existence ever in the process of creating, and if you delight in beauty, mystery, and wonder, you will dance with Daniel through the four relationships of regeneration—chaos, bounds, art, and singularity—as *Dark Cloud Country* delights your mind and dazzles your spirit."

—FRED PROVENZA
Professor emeritus, behavioral ecology,
Utah State University; author of *Nourishment*

"*Dark Cloud Country* is a short book that reads like a long one. Carefully we must walk through Griffith's words to find the nourishment our souls require. *Dark Cloud Country* is written in a language that digs through the innermost being, like a sacred encounter—the kind your keep closed somewhere special in your heart. Griffith's words are a great call, a nudge, a whisper, and a tap on the shoulder for all of us to remember the essence of regeneration: a beautiful story."

—PRECIOUS PHIRI
Co-Founder of Igugu Trust,
African Coordinator for Regeneration International,
educator and farmer in Hwange Community, Zimbabwe

"*Dark Cloud Country* captivates us and stirs our souls. I finished the book yearning for more but realizing that I could find more simply by embracing life!"

—GABE BROWN
Author of *Dirt to Soil*

"An eco-poet and philosopher, Griffith's ecstatic imaginings and lyrical prose don't just live on the page, they pulse in the body, calling us back into right relationship with our beautiful and ever-bewitching home planet. Myth and rumination, physics and ritual, soil and soul all converge, here, to give voice to the magnificence of life. Reading *Dark Cloud Country* is like watching a murmuration of starlings. The mind swerves. Dives. Rises. It travels to surprising places. The heart too."

—MARY REYNOLDS THOMPSON

Author of *Reclaiming the Wild Soul* and *A Wild Soul Woman*

"We could say that wilding—poet-essayist Daniel Griffith's more mundane professional occupation—is a mystical way to interact with the land: not to see earth as separate, yielding produce only when forced through labour, but earth as a creative whole, an unfathomable totality which requires that everyone and everything (including the gardener) makes themselves edible in order to partake in the bounty of growth and fruit. With Dark Cloud Country, Griffith has written prose that equals the wild itself—an entangled whole that is ever growing and only yielding fruit if the reader lets go of their illusion of being able to control its aliveness."

—ANDREAS WEBER

Biologist, philosopher, and author of *The Biology of Wonder* and *Matter and Desire*

"In the beginning, it was Daniel's voice echoing in my head when I followed the lines. But then, gradually, it became mine. The more I read it out loud, the more it resonated within me and resonated with my voice. The jump between story, poem, and lyrical prose broke my flow and I was startled into a deep awareness. I often had to pause to look out of my window to practice my own observations. The more I read, the less notes I took. The more I just am—sitting with the words ringing in my head. Griffith's *Dark Cloud Country* make it clear—it is art we lack, not science; poems, not progress."

—LEON BUCHER

HUB Lead of Landregeneration, Germany

"Daniel Griffith's *Dark Cloud Country* isn't your typical how-to save the planet guide. Instead, it proposes an antidote to the way we live our lives as individuals. *Dark Cloud Country* is a thought-provoking challenge to the stories we tell ourselves. Open up and let Griffith's words flow through you. You might be surprised what you find."

—ANTHONY GUSTIN DC, MS

Host of The Natural State Podcast author of Keto Answers

"Daniel Griffith's incantations don't attempt to merely teach, discover, or inspire; instead, he invites us to remember ourselves in an intimate dance with creation. Griffith guides our departure from the noisy shores of theory to a quiet stillness—a place where we perceive an ancient melody rise and begin to dance again. At once familiar and confronting, *Dark Cloud Country* is a deep well of wisdom whose waters I will no doubt draw from for many years to come."

—DAVID LEON

Co-Founder and Executive Director of Farmer's Footprint

"*Dark Cloud Country* is a magical, artful meditation on what it means to be human in the here-and-now: a salve to the excruciating buzzing of a civilization composting around us. It's a request to sit still and listen to all that circumambulates us through all timelines. It is a love-letter to lineage, togetherness, and all magic that can be gleaned from rootedness and relationship. It is a song for the death that unites us all."

—MAREN MORGAN

Writer/Filmmaker/Podcaster and Co-creator of Death in The Garden

"Like a brilliant mind wandering amidst beautiful chaos, Griffith explores the depths of regeneration through an outcry for observation, of ourselves first and our surroundings second. *Dark Cloud Country* is a necessary and beautiful wayfinding expedition to get lost in our musings toward a definition of what Regeneration *actually* means—it is an invitation to love, to choose, and to do better. This is a work that starts in Griffith's words and concludes deep within our hearts."

—JULIE JACKSON
Co-Founder of Taurio

"*Dark Cloud Country* reminds us that landscapes, homelands, and communities are not merely spaces to hold our invaluable quest for awe, beauty, love. They also are vessels for our despair, hardship, loss, grief. With all those emotions embodied, space becomes place and place is protagonist. Daniel's words, which he encourages us to voice on our own through reading the text, meld with so many before us, creating the relationships necessary for regeneration."

—ANDREA MALMBERG
Savory Institute Master Field Professional
Ecological Outcome Master Verifier

"*Dark Cloud Country* is a beautiful dive into the subject of regeneration from ecological, spiritual, scientific, and philosophical perspectives. In lyrical, meditative prose, Griffith invites readers to expand their understanding of regenerative living and thinking."

—STEPHANIE ANDERSON
Author of *One Size Fits None*

"Reading Daniel's writing reminds me that our teachers come in all forms. For him, in *Dark Cloud Country*, it is the oaks, the soil, the sunlight, the numbers, the language, the ancestral stories, and of course community. And for me, Daniel is a teacher, or perhaps a translator. Maybe both. . . . Daniel's writing is vital to changing the way we perceive and thus behave toward each other and the natural world. If we do not stop completely, deconstruct, wonder and wander, as Daniel teaches us, I fear the regenerative movement will become captured by the industrial model, and through reduction to a set of practices, scaled and replicated. And lost. It is on this narrow path between hope and sadness, between chaos and order, that Daniel leads us. The forest, with its life/death/life cycle, and its community is there, he teaches, if only we can learn to see it."

—ABBEY KINGDON-SMITH

Savory Institute Global Network Coordinator
and Holder at UVE

"*Dark Cloud Country,* despite its length in pages, was not written for casual consumption. One may easily find that its careful reading is like falling down the stairs. Here you lie, looking up at what seemed a task that required no thought beyond the intended destination. But Griffith flagrantly greased the steps to produce an awakening that only a tumble down the steps can produce: Stop. Think. Be mindful. . . Griffith's words will neither deter nor defeat but rather invite. For, as the author himself states, 'Chaos is not disorder, but order beyond form.'"

—JEFFERY SONDREGGER

Conscious Agrarian, Husband, and Father

Dark Cloud Country

The 4 Relationships of Regeneration

BY Daniel Firth Griffith

A Robinia Press Book
VIRGINIA

2022

A Robinia Press Book

Published By
Robinia Press,
Wingina.

a division of
Robinia Group, Inc.
530 James River Road
Wingina, Virginia 24599

Library of Congress
Cataloging-in-Publication Data
Griffith, Daniel, 1993 –
Dark Cloud Country: The 4 Relationships of Regeneration / by Daniel Firth Griffith.—1st ed.
p. cm.

ISBN-13: 978-1-7354922-7-8.

"Unless someone like you cares a whole awful lot,
Nothing is going to get better. It's not."

DR SEUSS, THE LORAX

This book is dedicated—
to those
who care a whole damn
awful lot.

To those
who take pleasure in
being alive—
amidst
the pain,
the triumph,
the suffering,
the peace,
and
the pain.

CONTENTS

CAUTION

Fiddling Façades & Drunken Composers

I do not expect this book to be an easy read and neither should you. Life is not easy; grow up. Not up meaning out, but up meaning into. Into what? Grow up into a child-like wonder where curiosity triumphs and our modern and mechanistic worldview does not. Allow curiosity to fuel your attention and give over your time. This book requires you to do both. If this is not something you can give, so that we can grow together, please return it or give it to someone who can. Better yet, give a damn and see where it goes. You may surprise yourself.

Reader, the following collection is an honest attempt at saying something. It is a hard thing, you know, to say something. Talking is commonplace and familiar for most, but the uncommon among us arise when something is actually said. Not arise as though it is new from the soil beneath our bare feet but arise as the ascension of what we already know into that holy sanctuary, tinseled in the triumphal sublimity of holism—of all that is.

I write with one eye out the window. It is important to consider that this book was written by dictation and not the silent ponderings and careful typing of the solitary author. It is therefore best read out loud, for it was written out loud and its rhythms and rhymes are best understood when they are let out in the loud atmosphere of your senses. Read this like you would read poetry, for that is what it is, although it is masked behind the mystery of paragraphed prose. See the symbols and their words on the page, taste their succinct succulence in your mouth, hear their bright balladry within the undulating rhymes, and smell the normalcy all around you. This book was meant to be spoken.

This book is broken out into what I call the four relationships of regeneration and each section—or *Relationship*—is constructed by an introductory essay followed by poetry and lyrical prose that attempt an enigmatic elucidation of the key idea. The essays are thick and heavy, and—while my editor did her very best to help me simplify them—some concepts have obstinately demonstrated their non-extrudable natures.

Before we know where we are to go together, it is important to know where I have been. The following work is an outpouring of my ancestors, and I give credit to them who knew plainly what I only faintly taste today. I am the grandchild of ancient Croats, mystical and unknown peoples from Eastern and Northern Europe whose Slavic mysticism the Romans sought to destroy and whose traditions are only today being reborn—not reborn, reawakened. This book is my attempt to connect with them, but not by transporting myself to another place, but here—I am here, in this place, in this time. Cosmogonic, this book aims not just to teach, but to be lived with.

Today, due to the many wars of yesteryear, I live far from the Croat's ancient homeland and occupy the ancient lands of the Monacan Nation, an Indigenous people that, instead of confronting the conflict of cultures in the sixteenth and seventeenth centuries, receded before it. The Monacan people seemingly had no time for those who came plundering for gold and riches and power, and I do not blame them. My ancestors left their lands for similar reasons. Unlike other tribes of the American eastern coast, the Monacan people did not share any of their town or river or place names with colonial mapmakers after 1612. Perhaps they knew that the English language was not yet ready or rich enough to carry the magical gifts of their ageless and free world. I do not believe that it is ready still, but it is *my* language and I use it to the best of my modern abilities.

The subtitle of this book is *The 4 Relationships of Regeneration*. How very modern of me to give you a list to formulate your life around. But it is a fine list, and I give it to you as a gift. All you have to do is cherish it, make it your own, and it will emerge in a timely abundance.

This collection of poems and prose, which really just wants to be poems, is a collection about uncommon things—things that ascend in the pain and the glory and the pain once more. Perhaps, in that way, this collection is entirely common—that which echoes through all of us must first be enunciated by us. Echoes begin with simple words and simple words begin with quietness. In that way, echoes and that which is echoed are both common and uncommon congruently. Isn't that what it means to be alive? Death brings new life, but for death to usher any life at all, it must first foster that which is living to die. The summer's flowers erupt from the sepulcher of spring—they rise when the frost-born allium's star-shaped and coral-colored beauty falls. They rise when spring dies. Life is found in life; death is just the echo. This seems uncommonly common and entirely uncomfortable.

In *Sh'mot* (שְׁמוֹת) the second book of the Torah, Moses removes his shoes when he encounters the divine made earthly in the form of a burning bush. In the prehistoric and ancient cultures of the near east, the ownership of land demanded the owner to have clad feet. That is, shoes allow ownership of the earth, for to own, one must also be separate from that which is owned, and shoes do a great job separating. To step into the ancient's holistic harmony that we now call regeneration, let us take off our shoes and release the colonial mindset and paradigm of control through ownership and become an active progeniture of regeneration—and not a patriarch. A regenerative culture and its agriculture will emerge when we come together with unclad feet. Many times in this book I will ask you to take off your shoes—this is what I mean.

There are plenty of how-to books, but this is not one of them. It is not my intent to inspire a response. Inspiration is a problematic thing, you know. *Inspirare,* in Latin, means to "blow into" or to "breathe upon." Etymology, the problematic science where words try to describe themselves by using more words, got it correct this time, I believe. One's response to literary inspiration is entirely similar to one's response when physically "breathed upon;" that is, to abruptly change or alter one's immediate course but not their final objective. A sidestep in a long history of stepping here and stepping there.

This is also a strange book, I understand. Our thoughts will converge with philosophy, mathematics, computational theory, theology, art, poetry, and the foundations of the universe. I will often utilize the ancient Hebrew language to illustrate a point. Just as you can look outside of your culture for the treasure that the stranger and the foreigner may convey, you can look outside of your own material predispositions—that is, outside of agriculture—for the transcendent knowledge of the world, our regenerating world. Do not worry, we will go through this together.

Any persons seeking in this volume for prescriptions will be disenchanted; any persons looking for climate-change-combating practices will be disappointed. I do not believe we need more tinctures or technologies to solve today's problems. They are not today's to claim. Let us simply open our eyes to the wonders of the mundane, the humdrum, the commons of the uncommon. Let us become uncomfortable. Let us listen for the echoes. Let us be, as I have written in another book, "up to our waists in the consuming confluence where curiosity meets the transformative powers of being, of rising, of standing still." There, in view of the naked and sometimes all-too-painful reality of the thing, we can find peace and rain and joy and grief and peace once more, abundant and overflowing.

This book is about preparing for the journey, but it is not about the journey's pathways. Once we learn to open our eyes, our bare feet will lead the way.

Mary Oliver maintained that poems and poetic things are "love affairs" and their amalgamation of the mystical and the common creates a strange sort of magic. And so, I guess, this is also a book about magical things—things that convey courtly melodies in the common vernacular. Yes, common as they are. They are Mozart's Requiem dressed in the fiddling façade of the drunken tavern composer; they are power in the Crayola-stained hands of the child. This collection is an attempt at such an art, and it is nothing more. I have no idea where we are going and I have no clue how to get us there. I have learned many things throughout my short life and that I know nothing is principle among them. But home this book is in this wonderful world and home am I in this melodious tavern filled with drunkards and dancers and dances.

Will you, join me? Will you, dance with me? Let us together fiddle the night away.

INTRODUCTION

Of Brides & Clouds

History becomes written when we become literate—that is, conscious but unknowing. We read of the past so that we learn what we have forgotten, and we forget the past because we have the ability to read of it. Literacy emerges when communities and their traditions dissipate and history grows into the art of remembrance.

The ancient tribal societies of the Southern Slavs had the Volhv, or "Guslar" in their language, whose principal role was to preserve their history by performing their mythology. In the streets, the Volhv would enact the intelligible mask of their culture's mythological enigmas, riddling but never revealing, acting but never orating. Their instruments were symbols and symbolic metaphors, and the surrounding children were left to unbend the mythic mortuary mask of their ancestors. Slav is not a racial term but a linguistic community, rich in local variations and cultural nuance—a community of peoples whose people community made buoyant.

While actions act on the historical plane—that is, consciousness—beliefs are believable only through mythology—that is, traditions. *Priče iz davnine* is the mythic and oral tradition of the Croats, or Southern Slavs. Meaning, quite literally, "Stories from ancient times," this ageless and sacred mythology transmuted during the First Great War of the twentieth century into a collection of eight stories. Like the Volhv before it, *Priče iz davnine* provides riddles and rhymes for children via the symbols and structures of the modern fairytale.

History becomes written when the literate become groundless—that is, disconnected from the past. Perhaps these fairytales were written for children who were born during the ungrounded times of a world at war, uncertain and unstable, in order to help them unbend and unmask the sacred and stabilizing origin and traditions of their ancient buoyancy. *Priče iz davnine* is the buoy and its tales are the rope, and together they gently work against the modern and marauding machines of today that obscure the truth as a wave's crest obscures the view. But today we also live in times of ungrounded change and uncertainty and today the high waves do a great bit of obscuring. I keep these stories secure to my soul. My ancestors speak. Do I listen?

The tradition begins when *Mokoš*, the shapeshifting goddess of the earth, appeared as the form of an old wife to a miller in his mill. It was the time of the acrid frost, that dark and early morning of the year when the cold feels its coldest, not because it is itself cold but because the cold is leaving but has not yet left.

Mokoš transformed into an old wife and silently surfaced at the miller's table, the mill's door unchanged. She sought the milling of her summer's harvest to supply the Yuletide cake for her new grandson, *Sunce*—or Sun. But hard was the miller's heart. While his mill stood beside a woodland rich and mysterious, its secret spring-fed stream, secure and strong—a gift and the gifter—he demanded half the grains it produced as payment. "Not so," replied *Mokoš,* "for I shall not have enough for my Yuletide cake and *Sunce* would starve, his dawn light forevermore a shadow."

"Go away you old fool!" the miserly miller returned, and *Mokoš* left the way she came, a flash in the frost. The door once again was silent and still.

But the miller had a daughter. Her mind's eye had not been heaved by hardness, for when she was born, the woodland's fairies bathed her in the rushing waters that ran from the mill's eternal rotation and foretold the prophecy of *Sunce dever*—that at her wedding, *Sunce,* the Sun, would be her Bridesman, he who would give her away to her betrothed. And she had empathy for the old wife and secretly milled her grains when the miller was away. A gift.

"Thank you, maiden," replied *Mokoš*. "I will help you withersoever your feet may carry you." Blessed by water, the mill found a prosperity concomitant to the heartedness and beauty of the miller's daughter, who now was called *Neva Nevičica*, or Bride Bridekins, for she was the Sun's little bride.

Times passed as they often do, and *Neva Nevičica* fell in love with *Oleg Ban*, a warden of the court. Their marriage invited Wild Wolf and his mate from the uplands, and Tawny Eagle and the Grey Goshawk from their skyward hunts. Florid Flower, complete in her singular beauty, rose And adorned the marshy meadow. Turtle Dove and Slender Swallow came as bridesmaids. Light made luminescent by love descended upon the sphere of their union. The creative fire with which life begins emerged and was lit.

But their merriment angered the land's sovereign, a heartless princess, who in her rage, formed a great army against them. Covering complete the ceremonial lands, she sang,

> The Warden is a rebel,
> We bid him to yield.
> Alive shall he be taken
> That freedom loved best;
> But the heart shall be riven
> From his lady's breast.

A great battle ensued. Wild Wolf and his mate were the first to fall, their fury foremost among the rest. They bounded beyond the barricade to exterminate the *eyes* of the enemies but fell by the many lances. Tawny Eagle and Grey Goshawk fell next, their pinions shattered under the weight of a hundred maces and their bodies were trampled into the black earth by an equal number of horses—servants themselves and not animals known. Showers of arrows blackened the Sun and the waters clouded with clotted blood. All seemed lost. All was lost.

Breath became breathless as inhales became constant and exhales permanent. *Oleg Ban*'s hand hung powerless, blood rushing from its source, and ten arrows apiece fattened each of his men's corpses. Death transformed into a herculean and fetid heap. Heavy-handed hammers now beat the moss-aged barricade, but Turtle Dove's love for *Neva Nevičica* flew swifter than any arrow, death strings made animate. She made it out of the fray and found *Mokoš* in her morass and petitioned for her help. But *Mokoš* refused. She was unwilling to aid those who followed *only* their hearts and she perched atop the fray in the form of a raven. She did nothing; she just watched.

Bereft and now without hope, the miller's daughter turned heavenward, leaving final death earthbound. The heaven's clouds had formed over the field and they cast a divine gentleness over the pain and the plasma. Through the fog and the fray and the fright, the miller's daughter caught *Sunce's* blaze in its zenith behind his clouds. In pellucid love, piercing through that which pierces, *Sunce* replevined Florid Flower from the mire, and she once again lifted her petals heavenwards. Life reawakened. Beauty and its breath bounded once more under the energy and cover of the now darkened but not dark country.

Through the arrows and maces and hate and love, *Sunce* saw what *Mokoš* did not—could not. He said, "In a lucky hour you gave me my Yuletide bread, and in a yet luckier hour you sought me overhead." Turning to the raven, his mother, *Sunce* thundered,

"Heart of stone! Were the world's laws be carved by spite, what crooked pattern would pervert thy right!" He then cast Water down into the earth so that she from underground and he from above would help save the worthy marriage of love.

Fire rained but the earth did not burn, only the princess' men's minds melted in their helmets and their bodies were grilled in a pile, heat figures made singular in form. *Mokoš* from below opened the earth and every man's grave yawned and closed around them. Finally, coolness descended and *Sunce's* fiery passion—that is, *his* love—transformed into dark clouds—that is, *his* peace—and it rained, extinguishing every surviving hate, and love and its peace fell like water.

Early the next morning, Turtle Dove emerged new from the moistened earth—nòvъ in the ancient language, meaning "new and unworn"—reborn, yes, that is what it means to be new. She greeted *Sunce* and thanked him for his water, for today he would give away the bride, the miller's daughter. *Neva Nevičica* and *Oleg Ban* danced together and the earth, she followed.

This tradition is titled, *Sunce djever i Neva Nevičica,* or "Bridesman Sun and Bride Bridekins." It is a love story of Creation, a mythology centered around the singularity of spirit and matter, of the human heart and the heart of the world. This tradition and its mythology also teaches the four relationships of regeneration.

Relationship of Chaos

Mokoš is most likely a linguistic derivative of the Slavic *mokry*, meaning "wet" and *moknut*, meaning "get wet." She was and she did by being that which she is—water, and out of water she creates life. She emerges in the fairytale during the acrid-frost, when everything and nothing at all was both present and absent, known and unknown simultaneously, like the midnight meanderings of one through the darkened but familiar house, where nothing can be seen but everything is expected. This is the dawn-darkness between death and rebirth, and her Yule-tide cake symbolizes the death of the summer's harvest and the prebirth of the new year's germination. This darkened middle ground between death and rebirth is chaos, and it exists to feed and nourish her son *Sunce,* the sun, so he may rise once more. Chaos exists to feed the rebirth. The sun rises from chaos.

Relationship of Bounds

Neva Nevičica's blessed union with *Oleg Ban* shepherds a living and loving neighborhood around it—from Wild Wolf to the Grey Goshawk. Their love creates community. Resilience is diversity in infinite motion, but its promise is not infinitude. That is, *Neva Nevičica's* community is light made luminescent not when their individual powers triumphed but when love gave their community limits—definition and relationship. Community made in love and birthed in blood.

Relationship of Singularity

Sunce unites and defends spirit and matter by sending *Mokoš* into the earth. That is how water fell and that is why the dew rises to the morning's hue—to greet and honor her son. *Sunce,* he is rising. The tides of the battle change when *Neva Nevičica* recognizes *Sunce* from behind the clouds and his laws and patterns and remedies save Creation. Mischief, as ancient as it is patterned, the law's medicine provides remedies when it is observed, and that law is love.

Relationship of Art

Evening descends in its resonant harmony when the heavens cool, the clouds form, and love in the form of a dove ascends. The evening is the great drama, the serotinal soliloquy of summer that swells into autumn, which only a dramatist could tell in the artist's citadel. In the end, the *ceremony* settles upon the scorched earth and the clouds cool the confab between heaven and earth when *Sunce* becomes *djever*—the Bridesman—the artist emerging from the singularity of being through bounded chaos.

Dark Cloud Country is my attempt at unbending and understanding these symbols of regeneration—relationships, really. For what are symbols but the relationships between matter and spirit, tradition and its peoples? The essence of relationship is that the elements are well related, that is, made well when they become relatable. Said another way, we are not beings that have relationship—we are relationship; we are the harmony. In this way, dark clouds and their country are not the eradication of the sun—*Sunce* is always here. They are the manifestation of his love and its transformation into peace. Photosynthesis requires the duality of energy, that is, sunlight and its precipitation, and while we relax under his rays, we dance under his rains.

Today, we live in the human-etched world of social interaction and societal anonymity, one of boundless growth, depersonalization, polarization of spirit and matter, and the complete colonization of the self—yours, mine, ours. In Hopi mythology, the fall of the First World begins not when Eve decides to eat of the Tree of Good and Evil—to become a god herself—but when the First People surrender their singleness with the earth. That is, when namelessness and separation conquer intimacy and connectedness and when the songs of Creation are replaced by the ceaseless babble of human progress. Autonomous individuality and its desire for sanity and self-worth by self-actualization and self-care (this is the modern century) is not entirely dissimilar from the first Hopi people; humankind has long been inclined to replace the sacred ordering and structures of community and its collective consciousness with the autonomous psyche of individuality. People have long sought to be gods.

But Eve is here too—she has always been here. She has never really left. Her name, *chava* (חַוָּה) in the ancient language, means "to breathe" or "to give life," and it is her fated decision in Genesis to step beyond breath and life and to be a god herself. That is also the Hopi's story, and it is also our story. We all fall when we cease to celebrate the co-creative gifts of breath and life and celebrate ourselves as gods instead, and we do a great bit of falling these days.

Be yourself, the well-followed and well-financed social media gods command. *You are ourself, will you dance with us?* The Creator invites. Nameless, the mordant of separation etches the isolated surface of our tenanted bodies, the resulting art neither earthly nor heaven bound.

And so, this is also a book of woodland dancing, of whispers from beyond time, which grow thick and opulent and merry with age, like good wine. It is a liniment for the liturgical rededication of relationship, like two lovers lost in the lucid litany of lovemaking—complete and never impartial. It is a book that seeks to provide the ecumenical dialogue required to escape the modern mechanisms of control and colonization that perceive Creation as a material to be molded—produced and purchased—and not a community to be cultivated. Nurtured, rather. Cultivation is such a harsh and civilized and sterile word.

It is a book about me and you and the co-creation of a country so dark that its drought-stricken dirt transforms once again into rain-stained magnificence. *Neva's* battle is our modern and eroding ecological situation; *Sunce's* fire and rain are our hope. What I am saying, if I am saying anything at all, is that this is a book about the powers of community living in the shared and mutual mythology of interbeing and harmony, of clouds so dark, their weight, as though the moon, pulls life upwards.

Yes, like brides and love and doves rising.

RELATIONSHIP I

Of Chaos

All my life I have experienced happiness, except that which was not happiness itself but felt like happiness was there, just indifferent. She never really leaves, you know. Happiness, that is. We come into this world with nothing and leave with nothing, but what *happ*ens in between our comings and goings can only be *happ*iness. It is not a thing that happens to us but a thing that happens when we become alive—or accept the life we are given. It is an essence inevitable and implicit to life. Or maybe it is the place in which we are, in this moment and every moment after this one, alive.

Happiness' etymological root extends deep into the early life of our language and is constructed from the ancient word *kob,* from the Sanskrit meaning "congratulations," and is complete in both form and function in Old Slavonic (the language of *Mokoš* and *Neva Nevičica)* in the noun, *kobu*, meaning "fate." Isn't that what it means to be alive? To be a blessing to fate? Happiness is not bliss or well-being or contentment or joy, as the Merriam-Webster dictionary would have us believe. No, happiness happens when life is living and happiness emerges when we labor through the common periods of our lives, not seeking happiness as if it could be found, but by being fate's blessing and then by being blessed by fate herself.

In a similar way, I am not entirely sure this book is worth your time. I am not entirely sure your time is worth anything at all. It is not that worth is absent—she is here with happiness, and they happen to be enjoying themselves—she is just indifferent. We have long equated time with value and we have long made time a servant to scarcity. Time as value is a divergence from nature's simple order. That multifarious monotony—that masquerade of intricacy veiled limpidity. We know simplicity when we know its lover and we know its lover when we learn how to love. Agriculture and its friend culture, if it is about anything at all, is about loving and being loved—it is about living and loving those who live; it is about happiness, but it is also about language.

It is fitting that the English language exists as it does in these modern times. Her users and her used, we daily strive to build lives that misshape her elemental feature of self-definition. Humankind is humankind. Tree is tree. And value is value. But even elemental features require the commons, and only value contained within community may be valuable. Mankind without the valuable shade of trees burns in the summer sun, and trees without a mankind to value their shade become lonely. In other words, nature's monotony says that nothing is as native to place than place, and nothing is as place worthy as that which is native to it.

The etymological root of communion and community and common is *communis,* meaning quite exactly, "us." As an adjective, *-munia* or *-munis* implies strength through introspection and safety through place. It means a public office with civic duties; it means neighbors com*munity* made buoyant atop life's seas—the commission of the neighborhood watch, for instance. As a noun, its directive transforms from the self to the external being of all, as *con-* implies the coming together of brothers, a fellowship of many parts. Intramural as it is peripheral, *communis* describes the value of life. Trees without forests often die from loneliness; words cast in the wind are empty waves undulating in a vibrating but empty space; foraging omnivores without foraying capacity are demolition engines of the modern sort—mechanized technology with a beating heart in place of a pulsing piston; and blades of grass without the community of herbivores are empty acres of lost energy.

"Why does the grass grow?" asks the child. Discover this answer and you will find the furtive economics of being, disclosed only to those who are happy—those who are living on the inside. Not inside the community, as if life had the option to live outside the community. But just inside—that sacred bosom where simplicity is both received and given, won and gifted away; that infinite place that Mother Culture seeks to make finite, for only the finite can be taxed and insured and measured.

I have previously written that "to see is to see the remarkable." Perhaps that is still true. But I think it is increasingly true with time. "But why does the grass grow?" beckons the child. Grass grows so that it can more readily see the sun's brilliant energies, I suppose. It grows so that the morning's dew can once again adorn its crystalline meadows of glittered brilliance with tangent shards of sparkling light, as though the Sun King's mirrored halls themselves shattered under its weightless influence. Grass grows so that it can more readily see the remarkable. But it does not grow to foster it. The latter is value. The former is time.

Fostering life is not beholding it. One requires faculty, the other requires vigor. The growth of grass is a measurement of time, and the community of grass is a measurement of value. To see is to see the remarkable. But to *be* the remarkable is to *be* community, to *be* relationship in an increasingly lonely and autonomous world. The remarkable is about value.

Without the herbivore, grass is without value. Without the valuable cover of grass, the soil is without life. Without life, the terrestrial world becomes valueless and simply unhappy. The uniform diversity of the meadowland demonstrates that value co-creates the valuable via the tool of time. Time and value. Seeing and being. Grass is nothing at all. The *community* of grass is all.

And I cannot help but think of the leaves of grass as though they were the legs of dancers in the fields of life. Close your eyes and heighten your senses. Do that thing that poets like to write about and the great paladins liked to talk about: prepare yourself to *be* the remarkable.

Do you smell it? That fraternal wave of life that pulses through the pastured landscape in the spring's flush. *Do you hear it?* That eloquent equity of life's elaborate economy, extending through exposition into the personhood of expression. *Do you feel it?* That crisp exhale of the late summer's boneset or the acerbic explosion of spring garlic that ignites the stillness and unites the countless multitudes of dancers into the rhythm of the dance. Keep your eyes closed and breathe in, hold it and let it fill you with its stomach-stabbing emptiness, and let it go—a gift.

Time and value and life.

Dancers and dances and rain.

This wave, this wonderfully winding waltz, elucidates the secret of life—the dancers are *time*, the dance is *value*, but the ensuing rain is *life* itself. We need the individual autonomy of the dancers, contained within the coalesced community of the dance, to see the rain for what it is: the value of life. Time needs value to co-create life and fate needs its blessing. It needs an investment but not the kind that requires investors. Martyrs, yes. This is what it means to regenerate. This is what it means to be alive. Happiness is here, this blessed fate. But it requires you, the cabalistic community of coagulated beings—of spirit and of body and of mind and of spirit once again—to become lost in the winding waltz and to be born once more. Yes, rain dances need dancers.

Chaos is the first relationship of a dark cloud country. Grass may grow so that it can more readily see the remarkable, but it can only grow from the valuable seedbed of its origins. That is, happiness and its grass and its dancing demands a rational relationship with rootedness, with chaos itself.

Chaos is not disorder but order beyond form. It is everything and nothing simultaneously, and its power is carried in words, and their language is calculus. While this may not stir your blood, it nonetheless regulates its flow. Let me offer you a proof.

Theorem: *Chaos is not disorder and its language is rooted in calculus.*

Step 1: *Suppose that chaos requires faith.*

Our immemorial inheritance is inquisitiveness. The physician observes the venality of the flesh; the novelist studies the despair of society and its soul via the language of indirection, a humorously hidden deliverance from the "merely edifying," claims Walker Percy in his *Signposts in a Strange Land.* But the mathematician resists the flesh and the soul and enters a more tapered yet more universal and lucid world of change—calculus. Here, outside of the labs of physicians and the stories of novelists, miracles take the form of *functions* and intellectual objects become the imponderable yet sonorant keys of life, both familiar and unfamiliar simultaneously. But here also is the foundation of faith, for one might argue that the mathematician's hope that these objects' unique solutions will be somehow identified by the function can only be a matter of faith. It is faith in the function and faith in its ability to do what it says it will do. It is faith that drives math and it is faith that imbues our inquisitiveness with hope.

Step 2: *Let this faith be a straight line.*

Like a lost gravel road, a simple straight line extends toward the infinite in two directions: north and south, past and present. Life may be happiness, but life is also this straight line, itself extending from everywhere and to nowhere. How? Life is complex, the philosophers tell us. How can it also be linear? Before you had this thought, you had another, regardless of its sophistication. Before you were here, you were there, regardless of its importance. Before you knew, you knew not, regardless of your desire. Life may be complex, but the valuable complexities of life are familiar in moments—that is, time and time is understood as points on this straight line. Time is the cosmic conductor.

In this way, life is a Cartesian plane where the mathematician erects the illimitable by the identification of the unescapably unknown. To say that a point in this plane exists, such as (x, y), is to say that many other points also exist, such as (x_1, y_1) or (x_{-1}, y_{-1}). Mathematicians call this identification by proxy, a lively sense of each point or number with a unique identification, although today unknown. Does knowing instill life? To have life, must we be known? Calculus says no.

But the known and unknown have a relationship—that is, a ratio, or slope of when you go from this thought to that, that place to this, or from not knowing something to knowing something. Your life is a vastly ancient, geometrical landscape infused with arithmetical vitality where this perfect ratio ushers the formless into the form, and that which could be is named. What is a name? Names in calculus are the degrees of relationship, that is, a point's distance from its origin—the heart of the Cartesian cross, the number zero, chaos itself. Yes, names and knowing and their straight lines require a faith in chaos.

Step 3: *Let this straight line's heart be the inner-most heart of all.*

The heart of life is chaos, the divine quality that assembles all that is, while being itself an assembly of nothing at all. Like the heart of the sun where massless atomic particles chaotically jolt and bolt at twenty-seven million degrees Fahrenheit, life in you and life on the earth is the child of the nothingness escaping everythingness. In this way, the number zero is a metaphysical experience of a mathematical echo. It is a definitive measurement of nothing, the name of that which is nameless in the same way that energy from the sun has the name of photon, but this, our life-source, has no mass and thereby cannot be stopped. Chaos, the heart of all, cannot be stopped, only nurtured.

The heart of chaos is the essence of all that is, a phenomenological structure of consciousness when action and inaction cohabitate and thereby co-create life's coordinates, complex as they are coagulated. But the chaos of our Cartesian plane is submerged in a primordial and somber silence. It is the stillness before the storm, the reticence before the resonance. The air is still, a hushed breath saturates everything, but nothing is happening. Not yet.

In 1986, the mathematician Chris Langton theorized that order emerges from chaos, just as your life's line emerges from the number zero. This iconoclastic view ruptured mathematicians and anthropologists alike. The history of the human mind and the evolution of nature herself tells us that consciousness deepens over time and evolutionary adaptation heightens only within generations. Order, they tell us, is the product of reflection, purpose, and choice. Order requires control. *Live your life in such a way and buy this self-help guide and your life will have purpose and order,* they say. *Follow these six practices and you will have a resilient farm business and regenerating landscape.* Order, Mother Culture tells us, is a product of choice and one's ability to control and colonize chaos.

But Langton questioned this notion. If order is only a product of choice, how do we account for life's emergence or the peculiarity of particular thoughts or the energy escaping the sun? What if order and its complex yet patterned realities were an emergent artifact of chaos, a remnant of Creation's origin itself? Utilizing the universal Touring machine, an early computer, Langton developed a mathematical theorem that tested this hypothesis. What he found changed everything. His theorem begins with complete numerical and logical chaos: it does and undoes, it goes left and then right, it grows and ungrows nearly simultaneously. But given time, it *always* finds order—perfect mathematical patterns that exist in infinitude. What begins in chaos emerges with time into the straight lines of our lives, Langton proved.

Step 4: *Let the heart of all require death.*

Chaos is the rooted origin of life, of order, but it requires death. Life passes through death for rebirth, but rebirth requires chaos—that which is unknown and non-moldable. That is the scary thing about chaos, you know. Tree trunks may be tales told in time, but their tales are only told through death. Deliquescing, legacy transformed by the silent raucous of rot, is the canvas for the coordinates—the plane, your new life. It is that unchartable moment when life is neither dead nor living, here nor anywhere. It is when death starts to move, that maggot-filled and mucky motion that silence makes animate. It is the number zero. It is the origin. And it is in this moment that I find Keat's words in his *Why Did I Laugh Tonight?* all too powerful,

> Verse, Fame, and Beauty are intense indeed,
> But Death intenser—Death is Life's high meed.

Death and *its* chaos is the moment when both everything and nothing at all is all, altogether complete and incomplete simultaneously. It is the molten core of the Cartesian plane primed and ready to explode when arithmetic symbols the coordinates decode. It is also the dim and bat-filled cave where the mathematical *function* ascends and becomes calculus' standard instrument.

Step 5: *Let death require words and their language.* Analytic geometry and its calculus is the language of life, allowing us to describe the sensuous and soft with symbols and words. As a life's straight line may emerge through its chaotic origin into positive and negative infinitude, it is described completely by the linear function,

$$f(x) = mx + b.$$

These six symbols make up the great sentence of your life. Read *f of x is mx plus b,* or *at x, f is mx plus b,* this function indicates a relationship of possibilities. That is, the members of the functions belong to the related and dependent structures of its laws so that for any x, f has a corresponding m and b and when related, the argument x transforms into the value of $f(x)$.

In other words, the symbol x symbolizes a pronoun, a grammatical bit signifying something is known but not yet understood—that is, it is not yet known personally. The branded b bursts with personhood and symbolizes a proper name—that is, it represents the exact point in which the line passes through the y-axis. The modest m moderates this conversation with rationality—that is, the slope or the ratio. Lastly, the purely arithmetic symbols of = and + speak of the relationships between these figures—that is, the laws of the coordinate community.

Thus, this linear function is the enduring yet impalpable truth of words and symbols that co-create time and value, blessings and fate, into life itself. It is a language that can only describe that which is created from and extends through the rooted origin of life—chaos, the number zero, the cross-section of our coordinate plane. Its resulting consciousness is, perhaps, a tool of that original structure—that is, chaos—and gives reality a dose of the real. Perhaps it is this uniformity and conscious universality rooted firmly in the chaos of our origins that imbues the image of divine in the all of us.

According to the Apostle John, *In the beginning was the Word.* Yes, speech is the divine quality. *And the Word was with God, and the Word was God.* Yes, language both manufactures thought and is manufactured by thought. Time and value, remember? *Let there be light,* and the light became known. The Hebrew Bible, or Tanakh, begins with Genesis 1,

בְּרֵאשִׁית בָּרָא אֱלֹהִים אֵת הַשָּׁמַיִם וְאֵת הָאָרֶץ
וְהָאָרֶץ הָיְתָה תֹהוּ וָבֹהוּ [1]

Translated quite literally, "When God began to create heaven and earth—and the earth then was welter and waste..." Yes, the focus of both Genesis 1 and John 1 is not that God created, but that he did so in *a*

[1] Read, *Bereshit bara Elohim et hashamayim ve'et ha'aretz va'aretz hitah tohu v'vohu.*

beginning—his *work's* beginning, *Bereshit* (בְּרֵאשִׁית) the chaos, the welter waste.

Chaos is the feminine emerging and erupting in the commonplace. Grief and glitter and glory—the silence of the womb that emerges as the screams of childbirth. *In sterquiliniis invenitur*—in filth it will be found. In the biblical Genesis, *elohim's* first act of creation is *v'ruach elohim* (וְרוּחַ אֱלֹהִים) a feminine noun that means "divine spirit" or "wind." Chaos' power is this feminine spirit, that which moves over the surface of the deep in two directions—our straight line. Mary Oliver claims that "the world's otherness is antidote to confusion," and I think that is also true for chaos. If we are to regenerate this world, if regeneration is the antidote to desertification and social dilapidation, then it must be founded and writ in chaos. What I am saying, if I am saying anything at all, is that words and their symbols have the power to create because they first are created from and are rooted in the great origin—the chaos.

∴ *Chaos is the faith that the straight lines of our valuable lives are and forever will be nourished over time in the massless heart of energy herself and require death and words to conduct this cosmic symphony into sustained richness, and this language is calculus.*

Chaos is the dawn-darkness of *Mokoš*, that acrid and frosted marsh where potential is unbounded and the emerging reality yet unknown. It is not disorder but order beyond form. Or, in Langton's case, it is order—just not yet. Yes, *Bereshit* (בְּרֵאשִׁית). It is that which is neither earthly nor heaven bound but heaven itself. Chaos and its photons is happiness dancing.

In that way, the singular and symbolic and straight rhythm of language extends through chaos to consume her many dancers, autonomous in their asseveration but subservient in their steps. Inundated, the dancers one by one become denizens of dance and members of the *function* and become one by one complete—stepped coordinates in their life's slope. The dance's passions rise and harmonize, becoming singular when the energies of chaos solidify into the line itself—when the energy is received. Chaos is life's community co-creating a communion of coordinates so rich, so total, so complete, that its gloried and gooeyed gob transforms, if only for the moment, into the full dance of life, that blessed fate—happiness itself. Chaos is the rootedness and origin of a dark cloud country.

O N E

The Dancing Dawn-Darkness

The morning, still, silent.
An absence of something I did not know I have,
wish I had.
Across emptiness, still, silent.
Fullness is present,
it is not that I had.
Do not have.
Boiling bulwark, here is the sun,
almost.
I am the morning.
It is not that I had,
I have.
The stillness, growing, grow, gone.
Not gone.
Overgrown,
we become.
And she said to me,

the morning,

as she held me

and as she let me go—

'Knowing is release

            and letting go is

                        finding

oneself. Not oneself,

                        ourself.'

The day.

The morning.

The dancers.

The dance.

We—

the stillness,

the verve,

the cacophony

of roots

and rise

and reclamation

and rest—

                        dance.

TWO

Stardust & Drunken Daydreams

How do things begin? Scientists believe they understand how stars are born, those resplendent spheroids of plasma and pain and gravity that our recalcitrant racket has altogether made invisible in the night sky. They tell us that chaotic clouds of stardust—or "nebulae" they call them as assuredly as if that is what they call themselves—form when another star explodes or implodes, they do not really know which. That is the strange thing about science, you know. It knows what it knows but even that which it knows appears to be unknown, or at least drifting toward the unknown. Science is like good friends who know what the other is thinking but often get it wrong. But good friends are important, and science is trying its best. It tells us that the death of one star is the birth of another, and perhaps, regardless of if we know it or not, that is the very best place to start.

"I celebrate myself," begins Walt Whitman's *Leaves of Grass*. Heaven's bard begins his earthly work by talking about stardust. *I am here*, Whitman is saying, *here in the embrace of myself and in this presentness, you are also here*, for "every atom belonging to me as good belongs to you." Not you, the reader. That is too simple, and simplicity is too mysterious. Whitman's poetic viscosity is an enigmatic formula beyond mystery itself. He is talking about the universal you and he is postulating the foundational cornerstone of civic virtue: commonality. He is speaking about stardust and clouds and nebulae and death. He is thinking about death and its chaos, the harmonious homogeny of life. But he is not thinking about individuality, as even the child knows that every twinkle in the night's sky is peculiar and named but is somehow most special in its constellational community.

Our friend is writing about the community of atoms and the commonality of form. Not the kind that occupies weighted tables, the kind that chemists in their Bunsen-burning and equation-balancing labs like to think about. But the kind that occupies the perennial contemplations of lance-leaved coreopsis in the summer's meadow, and the titmouse with its hedjet-hewed and tufted-top that neatly settles on its gilded roosts, if only for the moment. But such is beauty's bait. It is rest in the arms of community, but it does not rest long.

"I celebrate myself" so that we can be. Yes, heaven's bard and you and me and the community of all begins in stardust; we begin as I and me, and that is something for everyone to celebrate. But Whitman does not end there, just as the star's journey does not end there. His concern is paradise and that is here, not there. Stardust is just the beginning; it is life passing through death for rebirth, but it is really life stuck in the dawn-darkness of the primordial sky. What is another billion years of twinkling and peculiarity and homeliness and remembrance? Remembrance, a funny word to describe celestial bodies of exploding—or imploding—mass that are and at the same time are not either dead or living or even actually there at all. *Chaos.*

"Stop this day and night with me and you shall possess the origin of all poems," but "you shall not look through my eyes," Whitman writes. Life's liquor is looking, and the Cimmerian sky's splendor is seized when we learn to see through the eyes of all—stardust is required to see the stars. To participate with the poem's potency is to step beyond the poet, Whitman is arguing. Inviting, really. Yes, he is inviting us to a better, fuller, and richer life. The alluring truth of his poem is known only when we step beyond his eyes and dive deep into being, into looking—drunken in the daydreams of the night's rhapsody.

Stardust circulating in the nothingness of space without gravity is death without purpose and life without looking. But helium and hydrogen co-creating light via the surrendering of themselves to gravity's great weight is community via correspondence. You see, stars are not the fusion of finite parts, that is where science gets it wrong. (Remember, science is like good friends.) Stars are the force that results when the infinitely individual aspects of chaos become a tessellating network of light itself—of mass, of gravity. Stars speak to infinitude, but they also speak of a luminescence lit in the chaos of life and death.

Walt Whitman's *Leaves of Grass* is a poem about death, but it is also a poem about stardust and rebirth and chaos and life and the abundance found in being *we* by first being *me*. This community is the language of the infinite contained within incipience, the beginning of all and the all itself. To nurture a more beautiful world is to understand stardust, not as a scientist or a good friend, but as a citizen of chaos, the heavens, the glistening collective of you and me and us and you again. It is to be, the all of us, soaking wet under their sparkling tears.

THREE

Death, Oh Harvest

Solitude may be measured in degrees, but it is weighed during the month of February in Virginia. Its amaroidal and blue-grey wind bites anything still vertical, and even the Dark-eyed Junco spreads its frost-heaved wings in valediction. It is heading north where the snow is white and the cold its coldest. It is tired of snow that is really just ice and it is tired of cold that is really just cold-hearted.

Solitude is seclusion and silence, but it is far from emptiness. In February, a spirit-filled melancholy settles on the landscape, a near complete heather quilt of ash and clouds and reticence and the momentary flutters of snow, and the rising Juncos from their grounded nests they go, their job here complete.

In December you can watch the snows and their storms gradually work their way across the valley to the south, their advancing white wall a doorway into another world. It is one of those doorways that people like to stand in awkwardly and without much to say, but they stand there anyway and say nothing and try to find a place for their hands to be, their feet stuck in the *marais* of the white and enveloping marquee.

January erupts as the great glistening giant that awakens life's flutter, and everyone, for the moment, seems to busily grow once again. In February, the snow just appears like magic from the leaden fog and often takes you by surprise—the turbid and surprising solidification of the grey and gooeyed mist. But it is a gentle gift that can only be witnessed but never received, like snow on soggy soil. It is solitude, and it is felt most richly when your lungs are filled, complete with her stale and asper breath. Exhaling clouds, new worlds are born.

In that way, her solitude is not emptiness but space filled with nothingness, the great origin, the Delphian spring is on its way—but not yet. Breathe in; breathe out. Hold onto emptiness. She is working.

Wúwuchim is the first winter ceremony of the Hopi. Meaning quite literally to *manifest life's germination*, it celebrates the dawn-darkness of Creation when germination is potential but not yet kinetic energy. Unlike the modern and seemingly fun-to-attend medicine ceremonies of today, *Wúwuchim* allows for no tourists, no visitors—only members of the village, for only time and its community and membership may co-create with value the valuable community of life. It also demands connection in time, for, if you respond incorrectly during the ceremony, your body is dismembered, and everyone carries your body's many pieces into the night and secretly buries them beyond the village. No podcasts allowed.

The finite within the infinite, humanity's celebration of chaos manifests what is already eternal, that is, life in its sublime but all-too-often secret cycles. It is the mathematician whose faith the function requires.

In a similar way, February in Virginia is the manifestation of germination, and we celebrate with her. It is the shortest month of the year, and I cannot help but think of why—life is born in the spring, it grows in the summer, it settles into an aged wisdom in the autumn, and it dies in the winter. But February in Virginia is neither winter nor spring, death nor rebirth. It is the chaotic middle ground, the number zero, the dawn-darkness, the interim between life and death, and it is here that our story begins.

Only seconds after the blade found its mark, life erupted. The ground shook and the trees rattled. Birds, unleashed from their winter's sleep, bounded skyward like fireworks, their sharp sound settling on our senses moments after their acclivous eruption. The wintered and now empty limbs danced like lost wood drifting and waving in the moon's enduring macarena. Life drifted sideways and upwards and sideways again. Waves are stillness, the scientists say, and a still sturdiness settled in our souls.

But the wind picked up, out of the west, and leaves and untrodden hay whisked in the wind like isolated tornados rising not from the heavens, but from the earth herself—she was not angry, she was not even sad. She was grieving, and in her grief, a stampede started. We climbed atop the bloody and swelling corpse, anything to gain elevation amid the growing pandemonium. Not pandemonium, a ceremony. Yes, a ceremony of love and loss, of happiness, of manifestation and germination. Were we a tourist or a community member? Only time will tell.

The shot reverberated against the aged and tired mountains, or maybe it echoed against the community of ancient mother oaks to our east, three-hundred-and-fifty-year-old specimens that, if you look at just right, they are themselves mountains, aged and all-knowing and falling downward in their own way. What sound does a trigger make? What is a cow outside of their herd? Lionel will never know.

Morgan and I had set out that dark February morning to field harvest Lionel, the son of Lynet, which is the Celtic name for *grace,* and the brother of Lena, which means *light.*

Happiness, she is present. Her synonym his birthright—a blessed fate, a graced light.

The *Little Lion*, Lionel's horns were peculiar as was his life. He was sizable but quiet and often occupied the middle ground of the herd's complex dynamics. A bull, he commanded life's attention, but his spirit was meager and, in some way, exceptionally kind. His horns never grew as expected, one forever aslant while the other grew perfectly downward, as though it envied the soil and wanted to return to it.

It was a long distance to be covered, the middle ground. Before the last echo completed its migration, we were on the move. We were ghosts in the morning mist and began our ceremony hundreds of feet distant from the herd, for they were grazing, they were happy, and they were at peace, and in this peace the ceremony began. *Wúwuchim* requires the villagers to witness the ceremony at an elevated distance because the inaudible cosmic pulse of life that animates the ceremonial ground is distinct from everyday life—set apart, that is—and we treated the herd's ground in the same way.

Upon landing in the valley of the frontal bone, the bullet rendered him dead but not yet unliving. It completed its mindful work so quickly that it outpaced the forces of gravity, and the body floated in the air for a moment or two, a soul suspended in the silence. He was brain dead, the scientists tell us, but his heart had work to do. We sprinted, knives sheathed of course, through the muddy and mist-covered meadow that opened heavenward and landed at the feet of Lionel. We quickly labored to open his soul and let his heart finish its earthly work. It took us no more than seven to ten seconds to close the distance and no more than five to finish our task. We were not rushed; we were not hurried; we were purposed and long practiced—time and value.

The thick, ebullient blood welled out like red velvet and covered complete the soil beneath us. It ran for minutes, or seconds, we really don't know. We were lost in the value of life, and time was nowhere to be found. Lionel's eyes steadily returned home and were washed with a paleness that you have to see to believe, or maybe, you have to believe in order to see.

Yes, belief comes first. Crouched in the lake of life, we prayed. Reverent before the mass of muscle, we praised life for what it is—a gift. A final exhale, the manifestation of germination. Life was reborn—but not yet.

And that was when it happened. The dawn-darkness emerged, simultaneous with his life leaving, and the earth opened up. It has never happened since and I don't think it will ever happen again, but it happened here, in this blood-stained and February moment—the ceremony. Most often, during a field harvest, certain herd members will come over to the fallen bull and say their goodbyes. They do not appear to be sad but rather acknowledge the sacred and ancestral evolution of the predator-prey connection. Death has evolved with life, and they have always appeared okay with that. But on this February morning, something changed.

Happiness descended and Lionel rose, not in form, for he was long and sufficiently dead (even the scientists would agree with that) but he rose, his spirit animating the western wind and its leaf-gilded tornados. It rushed around us, and its energy animated the trees and the grasses and everything that moved. The last of the Juncos left their grounded nests, and the circling vultures' patience increased as they watched from above. The energy then gathered overhead and hovered just beyond our reach. Life seemed to float or want to float—or maybe that is the same thing.

A gravity descended like that of a receding ocean wave that pulled us down and tossed us upon the earth, and all was still. Nothing moved, and the tornados and the vultures and the wind stopped, a strong stillness surrendered the energy. After a moment, the energy then floated once more above us and then it dropped, and its collision with the soil reverberated and lifted the earth this time like a wave—up and down, and down and up again, rhythmic and erratic and overwhelming.

The herd's excitement ignited as Lionel's spirit worked through each animal concurrently, like energy through a singular wire. And then it happened. Their hooves were the energetic entrance point and they danced wildly all around us, kicking and twisting and singing and kicking again. The trees waved and the vulture's circled. The once-settled February mist pulsed in the dawn-darkness and ensuing germination. The dancers solidified and the dance became singular, and all of the hundreds of bovines and trees and birds joined the western wind's tornado and completed three perfect and circular rotations around us and Lionel, and then all came to an abrupt and nearly complete halt. A perfectly silent stillness suspended across the scorched earth and the dust settled slowly. Like a cavalry around an object, everyone faced us in the middle, and no one breathed. The earth closed and a calf walked beyond the muddled mass and approached us. It was a month-old bull calf, the youngest animal in the herd, and he was everything at once—grief and glory and glitter.

He walked within a few feet of us and never looked away. Calves are shy and often do not trust humans, those unsteady bipeds that work so hard to produce abundance. But he trusted *us,* or perhaps he trusted the *moment,* and looked us in the eye and held his gaze for time unknown—this was only about value. Morgan was crying; I was scared. On the far side of tears, we met beyond where speech alone could have transported us. We were in the midst of some miracle. We were a member of the chaos, the great origin. We were where we were supposed to be and we felt expected for some reason. *Hello. Welcome home,* he said. We felt perfectly in place. Without diverting his gaze, the calf uttered a simple sound, one of which we have never heard before or since. His eyes remained fixed on ours and he stood there, breathing, creating new worlds, and then he departed and the herd dispersed. Eyes wet and fingers shaking, we worked into the morning. Chaos had germinated.

What sound does a trigger make? Lionel will never know.

FOUR

There is Nothing as Sure as Nothing at All

This poem may not be about anything at all—
but if it was,
then it would be
about the rhythms of the earth
and it would be
about getting off your bum
and dancing until the rains come.

Will you—
not be about anything at all?

Will you—
dance with me?

FIVE

Ivy-Veiled Boughs

He was dying. He had been dying for many years and I remember his dying well.

Death, a coarse chin, propriety abnegated by pain. A slow walk, a mathematical devolution of aged velocity, of position over time. A gentle gaze, a shimmer fabricated by his many years—not so many. A soft voice, a love masked agony, an instrument of immortality. He was aged but he was also dying. What does a child know about pain and war and death and the love that energizes passion's permutation into peace? What does a child know about death and grief and love? What does a child know?

Life, as Malcolm Guite writes, is a "mess of desolation laced with hope, communion with a whisky on the side," and I cannot help but think this is also true for death. My Papa watched me play from his chair in the corner of the living room and he said nothing. He said everything, but I had not the ears. Blocks and crayons and board games and cheesy-doodles and laughter—nothing ahead, nothing behind, just now, a stillness suspended in the serene embrace of youth. My grandmother—Nana, we lovingly called her—would often play with us on the floor next to him or at the kitchen table behind him. But we never played in front of him. Why? What does a child know?

She would occupy our attentions with some intricate boardgame that took a bit too much attention to master for youngsters to muster. Our eyes, orbs in childhood's orbit, would inevitably drift and float endlessly to the flickering light of his television. It was a gravitational force, and gravity is the universe's ultimate master. One day, his gravity overcame our interest in her game, and our attentions drifted in space. That is what life does, you know. It drifts endlessly in space.

This scientific law is the ironic foundation of modern science's theory of our origins. The Big Bang, the origin of life via the singular explosion of dense matter that somehow existed beforehand, cast the universe into perpetual and increasing loneliness. As matter drifted apart, the universe cooled. This solitary induced cooling allowed atoms to form, and life slowly developed. Life is the product of loneliness, the scientists say. *We know this is true because we have asked her*. But her empty, cosmic womb that space as a term of magnitude inadequately describes replies in loneliness. We do not know her.

Us moderns are good scientists and poor lovers. We classify her widowed response as "red-shift," that which we understand as energy drifting away from the source, and I cannot help but think of Nana's board game and her dying husband's television set and our drifting attentions. Pieces of a game that we did not understand exploded in directions we did not see, could not see. Nana had slammed the game board shut and declared my sister the winner. She wasn't even in the lead. But scientific theories are good enough and Nana had her own.

Nana was an Ancient Celt turned Bostonian, the fiery sort that made us chew on her chicken wing's grizzle until we gave up and swallowed it whole. The sort that took us children out to eat in Washington D.C. during her husband's funeral at Arlington National Cemetery to focus on honing and improving our table manners in public. The sort that raised five children herself, during the many war years of the twentieth century. The sort that would never pass by the opportunity to give a hug, a kiss, a snack, or a moment. She gave us so many. She gave us so much. She was a hard woman, but life and Mother Earth are also hard women, and they are also wonderful women, and their strength is kindness, and they gift it to us in moments. She gifted us with so many moments.

But he was dying. I have many times tried to recall his dying voice and have many times failed. That is death, you see. Something so entirely real but something altogether allusive. Not elusive, for make no mistake, it is coming for me and you and the all of us. It is the only thing we know to be true in this cooling and lonely universe. Death is as allusive as an allusion, a co-creative and emergent force that enigmatically transforms what is into what will be—the chaos.

But he was dying. Once I thought I heard him while watching my own children play in the grove of black walnuts which grow behind our house—a woodland that, through its allelopathic appetites, has long since wiped all memory of its ancestral articulates. We drifting and cooling and lonely atoms naturally gravitate to story, to place, to legacy, for science says we have none of our own.

Look at the wolf oak spreading its great legacy in the pastured landscape and know four-hundred years' worth of ecological and social history in a moment, a sweeping glance. It was born from the Mother Oak that herself lived during the height of the European Dark Ages. It sprouted in the illimitable freedom and protection that ancient briars—long eradicated by human industry—provided against the ranging elk and the displaced bison. It grew in the complex coalescence of an ecosystem succession and societal transformation from a dark age to one, perhaps, even darker, for it emerged as the Mother anew just in time for the modern mechanizations of industrious mankind to slaughter. It is argued by some that only eight percent of the forests of the Eastern United States survived the industrious logging of the early-to mid-twentieth century. Our Mother Oak grew close to this grove of black walnuts and survived this period, although I am sure she has felt and continues to feel quite lonely, wouldn't you?

But the black walnuts stand in happy isolation. Perhaps they would agree with modern scientists on their origin theories. Perhaps, they are too busy to care. Look at this grove and know only what lives in the now, today. Yes, this is the perfect place for children to play, to learn, to grow. For children time is endless, and the value of the moment is laughter.

Black walnuts commit allelopathy, which means, "death to others," although modern ecologists choose the more kindred phrase, "soil-mediated chemical interference." Even scientists are afraid of talking about death and so they call it "interference," as if soil-born toxic chemical agents that destroy competing life is just "interference" or meddling. Allelopathy is first degree murder in the plant world, and the black walnut commits the crime when it releases juglone from its roots, a poison intended to eradicate competition.

But memorials they are. Memorials are funny things, you know. They date that which has nothing to do with time and singularize that which only occurs in the community of life—the individual. Perhaps it was the grove that was talking; perhaps the voice I heard was just the wind finding its way through their ivy-veiled boughs; perhaps my Papa had come to visit from his chair in the corner of that living room. But it was no good; we were too busy playing to take full notice. We were too busy playing and too busy watching the ivy grow downwards like weighted iron, anchoring us to this place, this moment. Sticks and stones and maggot-filled walnut hulls and summer shade and poison ivy closing in—everything ahead, nothing behind—childishness cloaked in the consonance of the common, of community itself.

I think it was just the wind, for it arrived but it did not stay. Even whispers linger in memory, their unexpected weight saturating the surroundings for a moment or two with potency. But it never really arrived. It just passed by. Perhaps it was comparable to a river, that which moves from yesterday to tomorrow without caring to define it. But it took me with it, definitions be damned. Was it a river? Forget the whispers and the wind and the river, it was nothing real at all. It emanated from death's chair in the corner of the living room that said nothing and said everything. What does a child know?

Seeking and finding. Hearing and being. To seek is to wander, to find is to wonder. Language, like memorials, is a funny thing. It is internal as much as it is external—it comes from within us as much as we emerge out of it. The only difference between wandering and wondering is two letters—a play on "A" and "O."

Turn the letter "A" upside down and behold the horned head of an ox, a symbol of brute force—the clod-buster, the honest and the hardworking, a zodiac of patient persistence. It was introduced into our alphabet some four thousand years ago, but its potent polemic is enduringly present.

The ocular of opportunity and curiosity, the letter "O," is derived from ancient pastoralists that predate the agricultural revolution and the Anthropocene—the age in which humankind, a member and co-creator of the world, transformed into mankind, the architect, the despot of the world itself. Progressing through Phoenicia, the guttural "ayin" (ע), which also means "eye" (עַיִן) in ancient Hebrew, transfigured as the reduced outline of vision itself—the letter "O."

Language is herself speaking. To *wander* is to plod, to seek, to inspect, to co-create. It is to be the ox. To *wonder* is to see life for what it is, a gift. As I have mentioned, I have written in another book that to see is to see the remarkable. Yes, I still think that is true. But sight requires wandering, and it is through this precursory and hard-won step that wondering (wonderment, really) is born. Time, value, life. Dancers co-create the dance, but the rain is life. It is through wandering that we may then wonder. It is through dancing that the dance emerges into nourishment. Ayin to eye, death to life, vigor to visibility. This is the wellspring of chaos.

But he was dying. My grandfather was fading from wars that had long been over, their raucous display now deaf in generation's genes. The forests once again grow on the graves of young men—boys, men, but mostly boys—but he was no longer a boy, and his grave's forest was yet unborn. No, not unborn—unrealized.

Birth is a complex and possibly erred term to use in application with natural systems. Birth is the physical reality of life but it is not the creation of it. Birth is the moment we acknowledge a life already living. Are unsprouted acorns buried under the moss-aged boughs of the Mother Oak not already oak trees? If not, what are they? They surely cannot be walnuts. What is the difference between the spring sprout of acorns and the four-hundred-year-old wolf oak's fresh cloak of spring leaves? Time—not essence or being or value. But we only see in time, and so I do not blame us for thinking that there is an essential difference. To be born is to emerge from the chaos, the dawn-darkness, the great origin, in the full glory of life and death and life itself; it is to realize the digenetic properties of life—that to live is to die and to be born again.

This is the problem of agriculture. We buy seeds in bags to then plant in boxes or squares or lines and then we pray for parturition while we spray for pests and weeds, not understanding that acorns need squirrels, calves need coyotes, and seeds need the community of the wind and the worms—and the weeds. This realization is the foundation of what regenerative actually means, and this is what an agriculture arguing instead for restoration wants: to become the ancestor and the nurturer of life's cycle. When we dive into the thing that is life, through life and death, chaos emerges whole. This is the forsaking of the Universe's loneliness.

Birth may be the realization of a life already living, but he was already dying. My grandfather would soon die from Agent Orange induced lymphoma cancer. Agent Orange was a chemical weapon used not to kill enemy combatants but to destroy the enemy itself, that which we cannot see, could not see. It was used in past wars to reduce forest canopies, and its chemical legacy is the modern agricultural pesticide Roundup, or Glyphosate. In 2014, American farmers utilized its powers to the point that nearly one pound of it was used on every acre of agricultural land in the United States. In sum, as though this great catastrophe could be compared to a mathematical error, we brought the war home and we brought the war into our homes.

If birth is the realization of life already living and realizations emerge from chaos, then birth and death share one fine characteristic: they are uncontrollable. Which oaks sprout and which oaks die in the soil is beyond human reckoning. To dance is to join the rhythm of the rains, but rains bring forth new life and new death, and this petrifies our paradigms. The wars are over, but our battles remain.

My grandfather would be buried in Arlington National Cemetery as a medaled hero and high commander of three wars—a man put up for the Medal of Honor, recipient of three silver stars, a distinguished service cross, and two purple hearts. But he was not yet dead; his wars were not yet over; his forests had not yet regrown.

As a boy, I was told his death would be painful. I was told my father would disappear some nights to spend time with him—to love, to hear, to wander through memory, to wonder with him in those last days. Creation is not loneliness. Pain and time, yes, that is love and it is not anything else. Loneliness cannot describe life or living systems. Said another way, love is life spent in the painfully blessed and often chaotic embrace of time. But love is not time in the same way that time is not value. Life is a gift given, and time is the transport of value within this gift. Time is wandering, love is wondering. Both require death and both are born from chaos. The sun rises. But not yet.

He was dying. Yes, but he was also living, and in this complex coagulation of being, between life and death itself, he saw me. He saw me for what I was—present and unaware, a child with no understanding of tomorrow but who was tomorrow itself—an acorn under his war-torn boughs or a walnut hull, rotting black the rich soil beneath with minerals and nutrients to co-create tomorrow's forest. There it is, the definition of life. Did you catch it? What does a child know?

On his deathbed, he penned a nearly two-hundred-page memoir and dedicated it to his cheesy-doodle-loving and chicken-grizzle-gobbling grandchildren—me, my siblings, and our cousins. There are trees in the world that die once their seed is cast to allow the sun's potency to penetrate tomorrow's puberty, and I cannot help but think of these trees when I think of him. To grieve is to see the passing of life for what it is—an emergent gift that, once opened, is reborn. We see it again, chaos, that is. Grief and birth, grief and glitter—they go hand in hand and, once seized, they are hard to get rid of without great care.

This attempt to reconstruct from memory is indeed mine to offer you, his aged hands wrote. *It is constructed*, he continued, out of a *vivid past that allowed me to touch, taste, feel, see, and hear at times that of the world I was born into.* We see in his words a parallel sense of being—man as creation and man as the co-creator. *Born into*, yes, we are created; *touch, taste, feel*, yes, the interaction of the senses with that which is sensed demands a co-creation with more than just life, but the community of life. He fought and lived and died so that we could be. He was the tree whose death cast its seeds to co-create a more beautiful world. Yes, that is chaos—it is everything by being nothing. He was the Mother Oak whose sublimity forced the attention of cutting steel.

What does a child know?

When he died, a forest was born.

RELATIONSHIP II

Of Bounds

As its campfire grows against the accumulating darkness, every mind has a story to tell. Some are of gods and the splendid morning's birth or even of ghosts and souls past, and other stories are housed in thoughts contained too deeply to find the keys for, and so they sit there in silence. Eyes, their yellowed and secret stories reflect against the darkness. That is why fires often crack and pop and burst, you know. Energy loathes silence, and often its yellow-blue and lurid and loud pyre of stories is not enough to carry the night.

An origin story of its own, calculus is the story of birth and its continuous change. Mathematics in many ways is the mystical study of stories and their campfires, of cosmic dramas and their drama of the cosmos. Geometry is the story of space and algebra is the story of symbols and structures, but calculus is the story of the world as told by herself, an autobiography of Mother Earth and her celestial supporters. In its simplest terms, calculus is concerned with change in position, a change that takes place along the spatial axis of a coordinate system—that is, a community of beings. This change in some *thing* is coordinated to a change in some *time*. Calculus is the evolutionary marriage of community with time.

Thierry of Chartres, the twelfth-century Paris philosopher whose work *Hexaemeron* examines the evolutionary origins of life in light of Genesis, argues, "The creation of numbers" is "the creation of things." Numbers endow life with spirit, with divinely harmonic breath. The harmonic frequencies of the notes in the Solfège—do, re, mi, fa, so, la, ti, do—appear to ascend in equal *steps*. But this appearance is a delusion, for their resonance rises in *multiples*, that is, logarithmically. Logarithms take large quantities and compress them. They squeeze cosmic magnitudes into manageable forms, and they are the incommensurable foundations of the divine harmonics and the vibrational visions of the heavens, the solfège. This is the spirit of numbers. No ceremonies or medicines or payments required.

Numbers also endow life with identity and story, names friends made intimate. Walk with me into a forest and speak to giants—plural and at the same time singular, for numbers make them so. *Hello, my friend, you, the white oak, your timeless story that we are just relearning; hello, my friend, you, the grandmother beech, your ageless chlorophyl made eternal through the seasons. Hello, my friends, you, the plural—the forest.* Walk with me in the undulating meadows of wildflowers and weeds and sing with the bees—a plural harmony and at the same time singular, for numbers make them so.

To have the many—a collection of trees or a meadow of flowers and weeds and bees—we must also have the ability to identify the one—the singular white oak or grandmother beech or wafting bee—for, without the singular, the plural loses its plurality. You cannot have the many without the one. But have no fear, with plurality gone the singular works quickly to be known, and the plural is reborn. In this way, numbers and their communities describe the infiniteness of being inside the finiteness of the body—that is, form—and in this way calculus is a splendid story of space and time, of communities and their members.

What do numbers and their changing natures have to do with life? So strong is our cerebral compulsion to subordinate experience to counting that ordinary English takes over our mathematical vernacular. *Look at that tree,* one might say. This imperative is also declarative—*that tree* indicates singularity while *look* demands our attention to it. In this way, numbers are elusive, and what they do is far easier to comprehend than how they do it. But we use them anyways. Counting frogs in a pond, for example, the frogs exist as objects of speculation, but the numbers doing the speculating are not objects at all. *There are five frogs in the pond,* for instance. While five is not an object, it is also not a property, like the frogs' color or gender or size. And so, what are numbers?

Numbers and their calculus are the adequate instrument for our intrinsic wonders, a focus for our campfire stories. They and their logarithms are the divine harmonies, and in this way, they are a welcome member of the human experience, and their symbols become the mythological homes of our stories. They are *Neva Nevičica's* blessed light that materializes when the singular story of earth—the cosmic drama—converges with the layered luminescence of the heavens—the drama of the cosmos.

Calculus allures the infinite into acquiescence through the ideology of limits, the secret mathematical nerves that bring lawless speed and formless space to flesh and spirits and their stories congruently. But what is a limit and what does it have to do with regeneration? *Patience,* our evolution takes time, and we must first understand the value of *continuity.*

Daybreak's preamble detonates when the morning's light saturates everything instantaneously. This exigent explosion of energy expresses itself as a global and physical property that saturates and soaks the darkness of life. The sunrise is a *universal* property.

Continuity is the mathematician's attempt to create community within this light, but it is not to be the light itself. Continuity is life within community—a union without gaps—and in this way, it is also a life worth living. This mathematical concept is a neighborhood with universal tendencies but local boundaries. Continuity is a *local* property.

In calculus, continuity describes a process in which members of *a* community—numbers, that is—swim endlessly between bounds. It could be said that continuity is a process without gaps and a place where that process never falls into remission. At its simplest, continuity is citizenship and to be continuous is to be a citizen residing in the commons. What if we put it this way:

$$\lim_{x \to a} f(x) = f(a) .$$

In the vernacular of calculus, a function f is continuous at a if the limit $f(x)$, as x approaches a, *is* $f(a)$.

In much more human words, continuity is when one thing is true in regard to another thing when the former thing is contained within the limits of the latter thing. A tree in a forest or a bee in a flowered meadow, for instance. Remove the forest and the tree dies; remove the flowered meadow and the bee dies.

Therefore, continuity is to be the white oak or the beech or that heaven hacked wild cherry in the forest of friends, and it is to be that buzzing bee that is itself singing but by singing it makes the meadow's colors enduringly buzz. Continuity is individuals whose lives flow and fade in the seemingly infinite depths of kissing roots or on the backs of fluttering wings within the ebullient but finite neighborhood of its place. Continuity demands a focus on *this* place and *this* time; it demands life to live in community; and it argues that, to be an individual, we must first be a member of something finite but larger—the neighborhood of a.

If calculus' continuity is understood as *local* members that slide simply between a certain neighborhood of numbers, then what are limits? Ah, yes. We finally made it.

A sequence S_n has a limit L if, when extended, S_n converges to L indefinitely.

I agree, that makes no sense.

Limits are the bounds of the boundless. They contain numbers—or members of a neighborhood—that exist in infinitude and grow boundlessly close to their bounds but never actually emerge beyond them.

I'm sorry, that just made it worse.

The secret mathematical nerves of change, a limit is wall, a value that you can get closer and closer to but never get beyond.

Okay, now we are getting closer.

A limit is death.

Shit. Now we've gone too far.

We've reached the limit.

The function $f(x)$ at a has busted through its wall—its limit—as x approaches a, if $f(x) = 0$. Said another way, when a function reaches its limit, it is equal to zero. At zero, calculus and its story of change lapses into nothingness. It dies, in other words—like the trees and the bees, remember? It becomes an undefined moment, an indeterminate form, a community without a name. "The creation of numbers" is "the creation of things," but zero is nameless and it is thereby nothing. The Indian scholar Brahamgupta's theory of *shunya* dates back to the seventh century. It describes zero as not a void but a domicile for the devoid, that is, a home for emptiness or the nonformed. *Shunya's* nothingness is not a function, for nothing and its chaos is the rooted origin of everything, but a form—unnamed, life is reborn from emptiness. Calculus's limit is emptiness.

Bounds and their limits are the second relationship of a dark cloud country. Calculus' continuity of limits empowers regeneration. It does not detract from it. It transforms the neighborhood of ecological resilience into an infinite community with boundless opportunity, itself managed and limited by chaos, that is, the silent vibrations of the great origin, the number zero.

It used to be considered that a limit is essentially a quantitative notion; that, as quantities grow or recede, they can grow numerically closer to or farther from "the limit." But the notion of limits is not quantitative at all in the same way that relationships and their regeneration are not quantitative. Is regeneration purely the amount of stable soil organic matter one has? What does "having" stable soil organic matter even mean, let alone look like?

Bertrand Russell's 1919 *Introduction to Mathematical Philosophy* argues that limits in their purest view are ordinal, that is grounded in relationship and not subjected to ratable quantities. They place power on a number's position in a series and not on the number itself. And so, what makes a limit? It is the point which comes immediately after the last possible point in that community, given the context of the coordinates. It is the human-scale or life-scale. Animals may migrate and bring nutrients from here to there, but they cannot migrate three-thousand miles across the continent in a FedEx 2Day air package. Continuity and its limits is not the eradication of technology or the eradication of nutrient sharing, but the eradication of boundless speed and growth that transforms life from the conscious and connected plane of community into the unconscious and disconnected fray of a purely pecuniary and capitalist world. There you have it.

John Ralston Saul wrote that "the conscious human holds happily onto a sense of his own ridiculousness," and I cannot help but think the same is true for calculus and its story of change. We live on a plane of our own making, a member of the local community of continuity and, while we may grow infinitely toward the limit, we cannot encounter it exactly. That is, growth is infinite but checked by limits, and limits are checked only by those who can name them, the Creator, *Bereshit,* in his work's beginning.

Yes, how ridiculous.

Said another way, calculus, which was created to comprehend the cosmos, understands the life-pattern rooted in the living soil of this world—that is, growth and its life is an inseparable continuum of interrelations and is thereby infinite. But it is not infinite by itself. Contained in place, regeneration has power, but only if it is limited. It has power if and only if it is contained in place and bounded and restricted by time. The greatest evolutionary changes only happen in time, not through rapid displays of brilliance. The birds of the Galapagos did not wake up one morning and think of instantaneous change, of donning different beaks. Even they understood that life has limits, and endless growth is a phrase that makes no logical or evolutionary sense or really any sense at all.

We see this same reality in trees and their forests. The rate of photosynthesis is equal among the different species of trees, and one oak leaf produces the same amount of sugars as one maple leaf, for the oak and the maple are connected and trade continuously below the soil via the great "wood wide web," a phrase coined by Dr. Suzanne Simard. You cannot effect a particular change within the community without affecting the community as a whole. Communities have limits.

What about time? Most scientists seem to agree that slow growing trees live longer. They live longer because their inner wood's cells, forming slowly over the centuries, are tight and thereby contain little amounts of oxygen, enabling flexibility in the face of life's storms and a general resistance to fungal diseases. They also live longer because they spend more time in the upbringings of home, that is, under the tutelage and nursing love of the mother tree. You cannot effect a particular change outside of the time that nature requires—trees take time to grow, and silvopastures full of fast growing and parentless trees are carbonic engines, but not capacious systems for long-term abundance. Time has limits.

Whatever the application, change and its numbers requires limits, for without them, growth enters abstraction, descends in worth, and declines in personality—that is, personhood. Prayer in biblical Hebrew is *tefillah* (תְּפִילָּה), which means "to judge oneself," and it is prayer that provides the introspection and self-awareness necessary to deconstruct our god-like and delusional pretense of limitless power. Prayer is, in part, self-knowledge, and its power is limitation made possible by understanding and accepting place. But it requires meditation, which is *kavanah (כַּוָּנָה),* the clearing of the mind and its business to enter into quietness—a word which is also understood as the erection of limits. Meditation and its prayer requires limits.

In Shakespeare's ultimate tragedy, *Macbeth*, the play's principal antagonist, the one who slays the great Macbeth who himself usurped the throne by slaying the king in the beginning, speaks of limits in his final soliloquy,

> Boundless intemperance
> In nature is a tyranny. It hath been
> Th' untimely emptying of the happy throne
> And fall of many kings.

Tyranny is boundless gluttony, and its foe is nature and her happiness.

In his *Almagest*, Ptolemy, the second-century Greek philosopher and mathematician, argued for holism. "The first order of business," he wrote, "is to grasp the relationship of the earth taken as a whole to the heavens taken as a whole." Holism and its holistic management postulates that life is holistic, that is, life lives and operates and regenerates in wholes and patterns. For you to say that you are healthy while the soils of your community are not is similar to you claiming that you are healthy while your liver is not. The self has identity in the same way that livers have identity, but the self has life when the liver has life.

In this way, life requires holism and holism requires limits, and this complex relationship is the first order of any business—of any change. Irreducible, this paradigm contains the calculus—do you see it? Holistic management is the infinite interrelations of our finite lives contained in the unequalled power of our context—our holistic context. This is a limit.

Today, we live in what appears to be a world overcome with infinite growth outside of this community and its context. Our world consumes beauty and churns out money. It is completely unchecked by limits. Do you want more biodiversity in your pastures? *Plant it.* Do you want more soil organic matter? *Spread it or build it.* Do you want to sequester more carbon? *Sequester it.* Do you want healthier grasslands? *Produce it.* But continuity requires fluidity and fluidity requires time over community. Can you plant or spread or sequester or produce without the calculable variables of community and time? Can you do these things without a context? What is more carbon in the soil or species in a pasture but simply more? Is regeneration about simply more things? Perhaps this is what is increasingly appealing to modern consumers about the regenerative movement—it is steadily becoming about more things.

Calculus tells us the cosmic drama and our drama of the cosmos is about change, and change requires community and community requires continuity and its limits—fluidity within the boundaries of our own making. The mother oak and that beech and that heaven-hacked wild cherry create *their* forest, but they cannot create *your* forest. That is their limit. And now we are back in the holistic context.

You see, to discuss change, we need limits. To truly change, which is what the modern regenerative movement should be about, if it is about anything at all, requires the continuity of limits—of bounds. And our Parisian philosopher is here again with us, reminding us that just as the act of counting endows things with individuality, so it also awards them their difference.

Calculus and its numbers are about distinction and association. To say there are two trees is to identify each of the carbonic forms as trees—this is *association*—but it concurrently makes them discrete, being that one tree and another tree are not the same tree and are, therefore, two in dimension—this is *distinction*. To regenerate, therefore, is not to count the percentage of soil organic matter or species in a pasture or the amount of carbon supposedly locked in the soil for a meager amount of time but to do these things by managing community over time—association over distinction.

Continuity and its limits, the dawn-darkness of our now smoldering campfire, our stories long hushed by our slumbering dreams. Infinite, daybreak's preamble nourishes our visions, and we undulate and float in the abundant and human-scale waves of a dark cloud country.

SIX

A Theory of Change

Enfoldment of leaves,

Her arboreal drama.

House of nothing,

The wind-roarer, its spirit—only.

Indeterminate dendriform,

System of limits,

The undefined, it is before—continuity.

Enfoldment of leaves.

Her arboreal drama.

House of nothing.

House of limits.

SEVEN

Love-Carved Lovers Live

I often dream about perfectibility and adjectives and grasshoppers and clouds. Yesterday, it carried me to a sunlit spot in our wildwoods that I had never been before. Aged stinkhorn deliquesced on its side—a decomposing spear thrust into yesteryear. It was faithfully employed on a fallen pignut hickory, and it unhurriedly worked to accomplish its eternal task. Infinitude worked slowly upon the filigree of the mortal and the mundane. Witches' butter jellied in the tightly crevassed and now moistened bark, consuming that which consumes, a parasite of parasites. On the forest's floor, golden leaves still pinnate held firm the vanishing verve of summer's vitality, and hollowed hulls were strewn noisily about. Nature never wastes a good meal and the squirrels in their compunction had long since carried off any opportunity of neglect. But sound was absent, a rotting ruckus that silence made complete. Not complete, whole. Complete implies that a part had been missing, a bolt in a jittery engine perhaps. But forests have no engines and they do not jitter. They just have souls that glimmer.

The forest mourned its passing friend, but it also rejoiced. While hewing humans prize hickory for handles and heat, Nature in her eternal patience knows better. Fallen trees also make for great grounds for the playful squirrel, dense homes for the burrowing beetle, melodious podiums for the winter nuthatch's metronome, anchors for the transitory mycology, and objects of imagination for you and me. They are the hallowed halls of the wildwoods.

Gently upon its great trunk my fingers worked. They passed over tired veins of exposed cambium, once energetic and white-green pathways of growth and life that were now a brown-grey mucosal mechanism of decay. They floated over the armored ridges of still strong bark, lifting and falling rhythmically but ever so slightly and carefully.

Change is community over time, and I was just a spectator. The created and sensuous friction was language enough—energetic, intimate, and real. Every passing moment the tree became less a tree and more a home, and that was okay.

Our heritage and increasingly wild pigs ranged these woods, slowly moving from here to there for acorns and nuts and grubs and the morning's golden warmth, which forests in their primordial wisdom conceal from those who move too quickly. But the hogs moved slowly, and I followed in their steps.

We often find our woodland pigs fat and happy not under oaks and hickories but poplars and gums and wild cherries, friends that have nothing to offer other than their heartwood. Delicate deciduousness is their virtue, and their naked autumn boughs decorate the soul's diet and penetrate the primeval with light. They are winter's spotlight into the lost soul of summer. Swaddled, our sun-sullied sows rested and were nourished.

Woodland agriculture is an arithmetic arrangement in the abundance of diversions. It is a systematic progression of change. And it often surprises and enlivens and even stupefies those who move slow enough to see it. That upsurge of life under the decaying deciduous duvet or the perpetual pulse of the kissing canopies. What is initially understood as madness transforms with time into a composed harmony. This is the value of the forest. *Will you imagine it with me?*

At its edge, one navigates the frenzied burst of briars and understory shrubs—entangled and energetic figures whose conjoined passions are not dissimilar to those who all at once empty a burning building. They are running from something, but they are simultaneously running into something, some conjoined and creative passion. Permaculture calls this the edge effect, as if life living in this fiery frenzy, which is also somehow happiness enflamed by urgency, is just an edge that somehow affects something else.

But a force draws us deeper and deeper, and so we dance. Swaying this way and that, we spin our way through the blockade. Briars thwart linear movement, but dancing is not linear, and the briars' barbs are worthless in the face of a good pirouette.

Applauded, we emerge in the forest proper. The floor opens, the canopy widens, the basal girth swells, and loneliness settles, a gentle mist in the day's overture. Whispers deafen and echoes detonate the reticence of the deep wood's secrets. Thoughts occur in hushed tones, and we move slowly, even slower than we did before. We have no choice in the matter.

Perhaps this is the force that the edge's enflamed community is running from—silence. Lilliputians, we the meadow's mouse, the prairie's spider, the woodland's traveler, evaporate under the canopy's grandiosity.

I passed through the story of the fallen hickory and put my fungal friends behind me. I landed just beyond a dense community of chestnut oaks and just uphill from a singular stand of mountain laurel, those shade-loving and umbel-sheathed symbols of perseverance and neglect. But it was not the oaks or the laurel that pulled me to this spot. It was not even the pigs, for they had long since moved from this place, their impressions now cloaked under autumn's kaleidoscope and transformed by emerging lepiota, those ancient, ivory relics reminiscent of coral reefs. Perched on the hillside's mid-slope arose the reason for my woodland voyage—our woodland voyage—a force that governed all the forces around it, a supergiant in a galaxy of dwarfs.

My eyes up to this point had fixated upon the changing stories of the briars and the chestnut oaks and their young branches pointing this way and that. South, they told of hope, their terminal buds were preparing to burst like children trying to get away from the mother's hold. Some branches were broken and without buds, and they were devoid of this hope and whispered of the mountain lions and coyotes and cats that no longer roam and manage these woods. People's infatuation with neatness has long since eradicated these predators, and the oak's denuded boughs told the tale.

These oaks are story tellers, and their stories tell of growth, of famine, of predation, of pain, of conservation, and of hope once more. That is the thing about neatness, you know. In its end, as all things have an end, change returns in its full and wonderful form and things begin anew. What is regeneration but change—of community over time?

But towering above these new-growth novels, an aged American beech heaved heavenwards, through its alabaster branches, the dappled dawn hued golden the floor below. It was autumn's imprimatur, a melody of moments limpid as it was laden in the light of time immemorial. It was the Mother Beech, and it demanded my attention.

In that moment, which was also many moments and even this moment, I thought of loving, of being loved, and of love itself. Donald Hall wrote that "love is like sounds, whose last reverberations hang on the leaves of strange trees," and she appeared to be a very strange tree indeed.

Stand under an American beech and know patience engraved by grief and love and broken hearts and strength not in resolve but time, that four letter word that also means love. The Mother Beech knows that love is strength and that love carried through the many moments of life is not a better version of itself but the value of love itself. The vessel of enduring happiness, love and its lovers widely diffuse their familiar boughs, providing a hug to the hapless and a troupe to the traveler. It is home (another blessed four letter word), and in this home, change patiently transforms community and time simultaneously.

Carved lovers in their love live, the Mother Beech said.

The beechdrops below quivered, and from her roots she handed me a dulled shard of quartzite from below my feet. It was faded and used and it was plain, something full of weight but entirely forgettable. Quartzite is usually a jagged and sharp stone, but this one was smooth, and its edges were worn down and soft. If she would not have handed it to me, I would not have seen it. Its rounded edges were dulled by the ageless hands of woodland lovers. I was not her first, and I would not be her last. I held her gift gently, my fingers trembling under its burden, that strange utensil of metamorphism, of heat and pressure, of sandstone made final in the arms and embrace of love.

It is childishness, you know, the thing you are looking for, she said.

I did not know that I was looking for anything, but the dream knew and she knew.

The child in its childishness is simplicity, for they are naturally simple. And they have no secrets, only souls that shimmer. Shimmer, that is, with the serene glory of scintillation, that moment, that flash of light that white-garbed physicists like to talk about. Do talk about—when the transparent becomes the apparent, and the radiation of fluorescence becomes the radiance of flowers. That is, when beauty becomes beautifully real. What the physicist is saying is that the child is life's floriated blossom, a *boutonnière* of the *boulangerie*. They are beauty and love and beauty once more for they are known in the forevermore. Trousers stained autumn in the fields of wildflowers—of youth.

But the child is also the one who is wreathed in autumn's beauty because they are first beautiful; they who lift rocks to view worms and not to build walls because they see life and not progress as eternal; they who obey the celestial infancy of life because piety and not propriety erects a society's edifices; they who live as lovers and love living because to live is to love, and it is not to do anything else. The child is the one who desires goodness for its own sake, and I cannot help but think that agriculture, especially the modern movement of regenerative agriculture, needs a healthy dose of childishness. When was the last time you walked in the woods? When was the last time you talked to trees? They are lonely in your absence. Will you go? Now? They are waiting.

The wind whispered as it winded through the chestnut oaks just above us on the hillside. A bronze leaf broke free and then another, my eyes were drifting, drifting, drifting, as they dropped, entranced by nature's pendulum.

There. Would you look at that. I ruined it—the child is Nature's affiance, she said.

The child constructs the civic by exemplifying the civil. But they do so with dirty hands, and they do so with clay and sand and dirt and clay, sticky as it is moldable, but they do not do so to create the mold. Their clay-stained inquiry is an autopsy into the soul of the world, and its verdict is worms and flowers and rocks and celestial bodies and humor and love and life and beech leaves and quartzite dulled in time, and it is love and wild hogs and wildflowers set ablaze by the sun's seasoned fire.

Yes, language and the commons and the community of words—the uniformity of life fostering the universality of being is the child co-creating meaning in the clay. It is love emerging and etched final in the Mother Beech's cambium. It is dulled quartzite. To be a child is to love so fully that time becomes timeless, that is, infinite. This is what it means to nurture beauty. This is what it means to have bounds. While the child's experience is infinitude, their childishness thrives within their limits.

What are their bounds? That is, what are the child's limits? Simple. The moment. A child's childishness may cause them to meander from here to there, but when they are here, they are perfectly here. And when they are there, they are perfectly there. More importantly, their perfectness is also placeness, that is, they love what they love because it is lovable and not because of anything else. In this way, it is the child that understands that opportunity and love and beauty are made infinite in laughter when contained within the finiteness of the clay—within a love of place. The child needs the community of clay to teach us the power of time, and childishness needs quartzite to teach us the power of time well spent in love.

But the wind again rose from the valley and the settled leaves gently lifted off the forest floor and returned again, finding firm their forever in the footprints of fungi.

Now, be on your way, I have things to do and only eternity to do them, she said.

Loved, I left the forest, the quartzite still in my pocket, and I awakened from my dream.

Only clay stains trousers earth-red, and only boneset's balm can clean it up—mend it, really. The child is simplicity, and such are wildflowers in the autumn blaze and russet-stained beech leaves in the forest's morning haze—beautiful as they are beauty itself. But the child grows and changes, and it seems that *that* is okay, as long as it takes them a good while to do so. A child's evolution has continuity, and their change is bounded by the moment—that is, community and time and love and being and the caressing hands of a mother beech and the enduring and moldy fascination of that pignut hickory. This is wildness in the wildwoods. You see, letting go is not losing control. It is the finding of ourselves, reawakened in the richly infinite community of love and laughter but bounded in the clay and forest of our place. If the child teaches us anything, let them teach us to be present, and in that presentness, to love and be loved.

Love-carved lovers live, and in the limits of love, the country grows dark once more.

EIGHT

Let Us Walk Together

To wonder is to enact a type,
Life's noble play that verve did draw.
Spontaneous the soul does sing,
But self-so is Nature's law.

Furtive is the passing way,
that veiled glass that dreams portend,
the bitter drink upon the lips,
being such itself a friend.

Sinuosity commands the leaf,
that waves and ebbs as it does grow.
But angels hued the autumn's way,
Tzu-jan (自然)! Yes, self-so.

To wander is to be the type,
that blazed clement that transitions bring.
Spontaneity her soil does will;
do-nothing is Nature's wing.

Resonance marks the passing way,
that timbre path her amber clothes.
The crunch our feet the steps do stir,
Being such itself an oath.

Prosody commands our feet,
that wave that ebbs but always flows.
But angles bound the morning's way,
Wu-wei (無爲)! Yes, nothing knows.

NINE

Patience, She is Dancing

The dancers turbulence force,

their steps in rhythm fault.

And man in party lose

what proprium has in vault.

The dance the dancers be

in erupting tranquility.

The rain the life shall come

by the pattern of the drum.

But the dance volition holds,

individuality there unfolds.

Not unfolds,

unfurls,

emerging in a world of pearls.

But the Common limits free,

this dance these dancers be.

And change, her rain shall come

by the bounds of the drum.

RELATIONSHIP III

Of Art

Out of the intangible pall over the face of things, a gentle but thick grace of growth explodes from the depths. Why it surfaces here no one knows, but it does and it does so very well. Her first leaves are opposite ovals that seem to cling like fungus to the brittle, brown stem. They are fragile and often hide beneath the oxidizing canopy of cool season grasses that wither and wane under the summer's new heat. Soon, she will transform into tall triumvirates of clustered triangles adorned with marshaled flowers fused at their bases. But not yet. Sericea lespedeza frequently visits this landscape when spring has sufficiently left, and its animals are ready for a good cleaning. She waits. Under the formless fever of summer's humidity, sericea triumphs and becomes the marvelous maid of the meadow.

Life is the conjoining of the old and the new—new species, or maybe old species made new in its specific surfacing—but so also is art. Art and its poetry is the conjoining of the old with the new—old beliefs with new awareness, old happenings with fresh metaphors or colors. In this way, art is powerful because she is a coyote in sheep's clothing, as she is a sheep that is somehow also a coyote. But sericea lespedeza knows this, for she is a phytochemically-packed and protein-powered instrument of pollination—she is beauty and health and clarity and creation itself. In this way, she tells us that beauty and lucidity may be intertwined in the meadow's drama, but lucidity is the temporary luxury for the eternal beauty of purpose—of her florid form's function. She is beauty, but her beauty carries a powerful protein. Her grace of growth, her marshaled flowers.

It is sericea that often draws me to beauty and its art. Many wildflowers grow in the Wildland, but it is sericea's great trick that captivates me—beauty's gravity subjugates my attention, but her phytochemical punch satiates my needs. Beauty and purpose, this is art.

It should not surprise that the diligent and observant among us are drawn to drama and its many arts. Liberality is not merely directed by constitutions or communities or laws or patterns but is blessed by art's education in private life. That is, art's drama delicately imbues a sense of intimacy among the general public, turning our often shopworn and undulating minds from the business of modern life to the mystical business of life itself. Art is the hurdle to the humdrum, a trip to the tireless human trades of hurry and toil. It has been said that humans do what they do and think what they think, in part, because of the way particular works of art speak to them.

Perhaps this is true. But perhaps it is more true that humanity's words in reply and response to particular works of art speak the loudest.

Long have I been in conversation with poetry and her pupils, and long has her greatest spoken most deafeningly. Who is William Shakespeare? While he speaks to us via the heroes, villains, and overall foolery of his plays, we never meet the man. He wrote no *Confessions* or *Discourses,* for his solitude and its enigmatic sonnets were enough, an intimate discourse of the private confessions of his soul. That Shakespeare speaks is perceived in his plays; that he has no need to speak is observed in his sonnets.

Sonnets are the secret stories of our lives. They are lyrical poems contained in the liturgy of private life, of love. They are sericea lespedeza in the meadowland that grows to bring lasting beauty through her herbaceous and temporary form, but in that beauty a healing liturgy she conveys—the cleaning and deworming and sustenance of her keepers.

Shakespeare's Sonnets, their enigmatic qualities diverging from the perpetual puerility of his plays, also provide a glimpse into the mystical and the intimate. His sonnets have no Dogberry, who in *Much Ado About Nothing* understands nothing, or Malvolio, who in the *Twelfth Night* appears pretentious but is the play's poetic pun.

Shakespeare's heroes become villains and his villains become kings—but his sonnets care not for villains or power, and they care not to entertain kings. *Shakespeare's Sonnets* are the heartwood of his work. And I like to believe that, while the sonnets were written *of* himself and *by* himself and *to* himself, they were written *for* ourselves. They provide a universal and lasting education of the intimate. They are the denizen's diary.

Sonnet 94 is what I believe to be the culmination of these private confessions which invite us to enter the writing and working chambers of the bard. But we do not see him. His shadow flickers on the flame-lit and flaking wallpaper that grows from the dim and recondite corner of his room. A wooden desk abuts the wall opposite the door, and ageless wax spills in waves over its edges. While we may enter his room, we may not *yet* see him. We have work to do. He writes,

> They that have power to hurt and will do none,
> That do not do the thing they most do show,
> Who, moving others, are themselves as stone,
> Unmoved, cold, and to temptation slow:
> They rightly do inherit heaven's graces
> And husband nature's riches from expense;
> They are the lords and owners of their faces,
> Others but stewards of their excellence.
> The summer's flower is to the summer sweet

> Though to itself it only live and die,
> But if that flower with base infection meet,
> The basest weed outbraves his dignity:
> For sweetest things turn sourest by their deeds;
> Lilies that fester smell far worse than weeds.

In only ninety-eight words, Shakespeare stylizes quite standard syllables into the secret soliloquies of his soul—of our souls. We need only to read the first few lines to witness the pain and the truth and the triumph and the pain of humanity's inner life. Locked in a room called conversance, he begins,

> They that have power to hurt and will do none,
> That do not do the thing they most do show.

Shakespeare begins his inner work with a riddle. Who is the *they*? Who is this nameless force that can and does not hurt us? What *they most do show* echoes like a bad dream against the peeling walls of this antiquated room, which itself feels like home, or at least we strangely feel like we are at home in it, and these words draw us with as much grace and mystique as they chill us with their cold callousness. Who has the power to destroy *and* does not do *what they most do show?* The sonnet begins with this harrowing yet homely unknown and then spends the rest of its ninety-seven words catching up. Are you ready for the chase?

Notice what our bard does not say. He does not say *but* will do none. No, that is too simple. That is too benign. It would mean that, while harm is the opportunity, no harm is the permanent reality. But community requires love and love requires the opportunity of hurt. Isn't this what it means to love? To have the power to hurt *and* do none? To give away all of your secrets and truths and pains and past lives to the one who has the greatest power to hurt you? Isn't this why it hurts the most when love turns its back on you? Love requires the opportunity of pain.

Community and its love requires the power to hurt, and it requires the complete self-limitation of that *thing they most do show*—the usage of this power. But it does not allow its eradication. Eradicating the opportunity to hurt is the eradication of love itself. It must be a choice. Love without power's opportunity to do harm is not love but something else entirely—something else entirely less everything. And what is love but everything?

And this is why Shakespeare says what he says, for this sonnet is about love—he neither limits nor eradicates the power—but opens it up entirely to the will of the *they*. Who is the *they*? *And will do none,* Shakespeare writes, meaning that it is a decision and not a directive. It is an invitation. A seemingly indifferent choice of words—*and*, *but*—that neither benevolence nor sympathy restrains. Is love power enough? *They* can hurt and do none; they have power and seemingly decide to *do not the thing, they most do show.* Is this what it means to love? But Shakespeare's room is dark, and his shadow is fading with the light. Shadows are the progeniture of light and darkness, but the darkness is winning and his shadow is fading. He continues,

> Who, moving others, are themselves as stone,
> Unmoved, cold, and to temptation slow.

Shakespeare places this *they* above the poem. While *they's* being is contained within the lines, their purpose is somehow external to the rhymes. *They* move others but, in this movement and maybe in every moment which moves, they remain unmoved like a stone. Stones are ageless and are delineated not by time or weight or color or shape but by persistence. Where does one stone end and another begin? Yes, that is their delineation. A stone is the ageless union of stardust that we call atoms made complete in the urgent unification of patience and persistence and purpose. Isn't this what it means to love? To be here, in this place, with a persistent patience that is really just urgency enflamed by purpose? Who is the *they?*

Shakespeare continues,

> They rightly do inherit heaven's graces
> And husband nature's riches from expense;
> They are the lords and owners of their faces,
> Others but stewards of their excellence.

Sonnet 94 shatters and shakes our inquisition, claiming that stewardship without the *power to hurt* is an echo of excellence and not excellence itself. The *power to hurt* and the stewardship of *nature's riches* are linked, they are intertwined in this great drama. Shakespeare is talking about virtue. *Heaven's graces* are inheritable when we become the *lords and owners* of our simple and small-souled faces—when we understand the choice of *and.* In other words, Shakespeare is claiming that nature's stewardship must be intentional, and it requires persistent and urgent dedication to purpose over time. It requires patience, and it is up to you. Virtue is power wielded but never used. This is the choice of *and*. Here, in this candle-lit room that is called conversance, Shakespeare is talking again about love.

But the room's tapers are now too low and their fading light flickers tepidly this way and that. What light remains flashes the shadowed silhouette astride not the wall's decadent trappings but the enclosing ceiling of the sonnet, and we recognize the original form. The new albeit fading light casts a new perspective. That is art's power. This is not

Shakespeare's room but one we know very well, for our old eyes the sonnet made new—who is the *they*? Why, it is you.

Art and its dramatist is the third relationship of a dark cloud country. To nurture is to have the power to harm *and* to do none. But the power is ours while not for us and that makes all the difference. This is the power of *and* and this is the choice of the human soul. Shakespeare's *Sonnet 94* casts the role of the dramatist—you, me, the all of us. It is the artist that does and does not do the thing *they most do show*. It is the artist that is the unmovable but moving stone. While speaking, the artist speaks not; while playwriting, the artist plays not; while casting, the artist is cast not; while depicting, the artist's portrait is depicted not; while building characters, the artist's character builds not. And yet, it is artists and their art that move us, compel us in reciprocity—or *reciprocus*, meaning quite literally forward and backward simultaneously.

But the dramatist is also something more. Shakespeare continues,

> The summer's flower is to the summer sweet
> Though to itself it only live and die,
> But if that flower with base infection meet,
> The basest weed outbraves his dignity:

> For sweetest things turn sourest by their deeds;
> Lilies that fester smell far worse than weeds.

The *we* of this poem is now a flower, and *we* have one more choice to make. While flowers make the *summer sweet,* their deeds can make them weeds. Shakespeare is talking again about purpose. In this closing couplet, he defines the choice—the *we* that have the *power to hurt* and so have the power to love must decide if that love is sweet or sour—a flower or a weed. Does it *inherit heaven's graces* or fester with *infection meet*? Notice that this choice is not for *our* sake. Flowers make the *summer sweet,* and themselves only live and die. Yes, but sericea lespedeza's selfless surge of beauty and purpose already knew this. Love's choice can only be selfless. Isn't this what it means to love? Isn't this what it means to regenerate?

What Shakespeare is saying, if he is saying anything at all, is that art and its drama is about love because it is first about the choice. And it is about you—the poem and her poet, the land and her artist, the *they* who choose to catch the pellucidity of the moment and not the moment itself. Love can never have; it can only hold, but it cannot hold tightly. Like fresh spring water deft in its gravity-subjugated descent through unwebbed hands, love has a purpose of its own. It can only cherish.

In this way, to regenerate is to be the dramatist—to step into the poem, to enter into the land, to sit in the room called conversance, but it is to do so lovingly and to do so with urgency and purpose and intentionality. Regeneration requires relationship, but not the kind that supplements the busyness of our lives with social calls, but the kind that is our lives—relationship is what we are, it is not something we do. We *are* relationship. It is to be the sericea lespedeza in the meadowland, the florid medicine that beauty enthrones. Art and its artist is not the conquest of nature, either belligerent or benign. To be an artist is to be this choice—not to conquer nature or do that which we *most do show*, but to have the power to destroy and then to make visible the beautiful and passing moments of *nature's graces*. To regenerate and be relationship is to be this choice, steeped richly in the full love and power of summer's beauty.

Dante is also here, and in his *Inferno* he writes,

> That your art follows nature, as far as it can,
> Much in the way a student follows his master;
> So that your art is the grandchild of God.

The artist stewards excellence by not letting *heaven's graces* fall into obscurity, into loneliness. Art is the recognition of beauty; it is to be the grandchild of God. The flowered meadow requires the all of us—art requires the artist but artists require the art. Regeneration is about community and it is about catching the moments' beauty but it is not about producing it. *Nature's graces* are hers. Too many of us believe that regeneration produces abundance. Regeneration *is* abundance in the same way that regeneration *is* relationship. And the role of the regenerative agrarian is not to capture beauty but to recognize it and cast it and then to lovingly gift it away.

Notice that Shakespeare employs the subjunctive rather than the continuous present when he writes,

> The summer's flower is to the summer sweet
> Though to itself it only live and die.

Flowers only live and die once, but their beauty, their impact, lasts forever. Art is the transcendent and cosmic drama made tangible by the artist, but it is not the artist's transcendence into the cosmos. The Creator instills nature with beauty; the artist elucidates nature's beautiful abundance but is not the wellspring of its weight. The artist is temporary; the art is forever.

Robert Frost claims that art and its dramatist intends to "trip the reader head foremost into the boundless." Reason may be the beginning of truth, but poetry and its dramatic imagination is the mysterious origin of meaning. Yes, this is the role of the regenerative agrarian and this is the choice of the human soul—to see truth, to witness its drama, to accept the opportunity, to have great power, to hold loosely its abiding weight, and then to trip headlong *into the boundless* triumphs and pains and beauties made and gifted everlasting in the love of a dark and clouded country.

TEN

Desert Dancer

The liniment of life,
the ligament of liturgy.
Sacred Holism celebrates
relationship's synergy.
What is this medicine?
What does it look like?
Well, you
of course.
And it is us,
to be sure.
It is the return of great heroes,
those common dancing types—
who convey choice's medicine,
their feet the soil strikes.
The rains have gone,
but the rhythms well our bones recall:
from vestige to verve,
we the dancers the desert foresaw.

ELEVEN

Flaxen-Haired Fairyland

There exists a grassland in the southeast of our Wildland that looks very similar to a grassland that you know very well. Perhaps it is your grassland that you see when you see this one or perhaps it is a neighboring grassland from your youth, when there was no mine or yours or theirs to describe the community of the sun's gift. The blessing of youth is the blessing of the pastoralist, those not so ancient ancients who ranged near and far in order to graze that which grew and not that which they knew. Borders and fences and prosperity and progress got in their way, but adolescence has always found another. Children are the secret salvagers of ancient wisdom, and in them, the possibilities of open fields and woods untouched by the overlords of profit remain untouched, unhindered.

In autumn, this southeast grassland turns golden under the weight of yellow crownbeard's eruption, and opulence becomes ocular as the child becomes childish. It has happened every year that we have managed this landscape and it has happened every year to surprise us with its occurrence, reoccurrence. The evening's orange light only enhances the conflagration of crownbeard's fusion into permanence. No, not permanence, persistence, for even stars must come to an end. Autumn, sunsets made ablaze.

What was a mixed cool and warm season grassland, dotted with persnickety herbaceous and woody perennials such as Carolina horse nettle, Indian currant, and autumn olive, now emerges in the autumn as a flaxen-haired fairyland. It is an ethereal but ephemeral wonderland, for it playfully lasts only for a moment, as though its beauty was just a game, a momentary tease of the senses. But it also lasts for many moments. Perhaps it even occupies this moment as you the reader, the imaginator, the child will it into existence. Will you will it into existence? I promise that we will never be the same. *She is waiting.*

At the deep end of this wildflower meadow's eastern edge is a grove of ancient white oaks that are arranged in a nearly perfect square. That is not altogether true. One of the trees in the northern corner of the square is a black walnut, its flaccid boughs indicating its senility. We have long observed this geometric community and we have long found this walnut wanting. Not wanting as though its gifts were lacking but wanting as though its friends had long since passed and it was lonely. Trees can become lonely, you know. What does loneliness look like in a tree? What does a walnut have to say to three Mother Oaks who were saplings before white was a possible color of a hominoid's skin?

Loneliness is linguistic, and this walnut lacks the lyrics. Every year a branch or two silently splashes to the soil. Foresters call this death. I call it tiredness. It is a burned-out star—a nebula, remember?—waiting to become light anew. It is death conveying community and nourishment to its neighbors, and it is a beautiful thing to see. *Here is a branch, my old companions,* it says. *It is all I have to give, and I give it willingly.* Splash. The mallard-colored orchard grass that grows under its shade swells and ripples, and then silence. *Accept it as my gift and let this death orchestrate your growth. I am tired but accept my tiredness, and let it sustain you and keep you.* Time immortal, the walnut awaits its final collapse. *We will see each other again. Soon.*

But maybe I am wrong. Perhaps it is just my humdrum humanness talking; perhaps I am scared and I see demise and I try to see something else—to believe this walnut's death is just one aspect in the greater whole of ecosystem succession. But maybe it thinks not of succession, and it says nothing at all, and maybe its death's gesture is just a silent act within its life's enigmatic purpose. What does a walnut have to say?

We often take Wildland Tours to this place and often find that silence is the only sound our guests feel is appropriate. What can you say when everything is already echoing all around you? Time inside timelessness, silence echoing through eternity. We may never know what nurtured this ancient community to grow as they grew, but we can dream—and in our dreams, we see a small homestead or village and the late summer coolness that these trees' shade so gently supplied. We hear children running and climbing and laughing as they ascend, and we see the welcoming arms of the Mother Oaks summoning their souls as they lower their boughs to scoop them up. We see happiness in place. If only I were a painter, I would paint what I see, what we now see together. But my words will have to suffice; they occupy the full range of my artistic abilities.

What thoughts did these people have, standing here as we now do? That is a silly question, for they did not stand and gawk at giants. They lived amongst them, and they walked with them. And they cared for them because they knew them as what they were: common. What sort of lives did they live? These trees know, but they are too wise to tell us. Time inside timelessness. But we do know something. These trees live and were let to live, and that tells us enough.

But the uniform Easter of golden flowers is calling, and this story is about wildflowers and not the wildwoods. We manage our Wildland's operation for the optimization of fall's flowering. Holistic Management teaches us that we must manage for what we want and not for what we do not want, and one-hundred-acres of worthless and unpalatable flowers that our cattle do not eat is strangely classified as the former. It makes sense for agriculture to push for items that combine well in dishes. It makes sense for agriculturalists to care about such things. But in the autumn blaze, and as we leave our manure-covered boots in the house, we embrace our role as poets.

Masanobu Fukuoka writes of agriculture by first writing about roofing and poetry. In his *One Straw Revolution,* he postulates,

> It is as if a fool were to stomp on and break the tiles on his roof. Then when it starts to rain and the ceiling begins to rot away, he hastily climbs up to mend the damage, rejoicing in the end that he has accomplished a miraculous solution.

Fukuoka's stomping fool is the modern reductionism and linear thinking that prostrates complex systems at the feet of mechanization, technology, and progress—those who shackle Mother Earth to benefit Mother Culture, those who see grasslands for their grass and not their flowers.

Science has the propensity to degenerate into this mode of thinking, but she is not alone. So also do philosophers, institutions, governments, polities, townships, communities, families, and, well, regenerative farmers. It is the witless piety to linearization that corrodes our climate and infects our communities. It is the clueless fool who, after repairing the rotted roof that he impaired originally, thinks of himself as progressive and heroic. What makes regenerative farmers any different than this dancing fool?

Language and its friends, attention and belief, need to change if we are to have what we believe we need—soil, that dark and iron-stained friend of dirt. Soil health does not matter, for it does not exist. The soil *is* health, and it cannot contain its definition, it can only inhabit its selfhood. In many ways, the soil is therefore a gift to be nurtured in community and not a commodity that can be improved or, God forbid, produced. Really, we are trying to produce health? How do you do that?

If soil could *have* health, then health is external to the thing, like this book is external to you although you have it, and soil could exist without being healthy (which it cannot), for that would be dirt and not soil. If soil could have health, and its having is the thing that matters most, then dirt is unimproved soil and rocks are unimproved dirt on their way to being soil, and the divine and chaotic and beautiful singularity of everything and nothing and everything again is also unimproved until it is *only* soil. Is that *really* want we want? Can life be *only* one thing? Are rocks degenerative until they are soil? If they are, then regenerative agriculture is going nowhere, for it substitutes reductionist thinking—*regenerative agriculture is soil health*—in place of an emergent intimacy around ancestral traditions—*regenerative agriculture is the reclamation of relationship.* We need a new language.

Soil is a byproduct of intimacy, and Fukuoka's fool is the sycophant of soil health, who in their attention to the part lives on their knees and completely misses the bees—autumn's procreative nectar just inches above their heads. To focus only on the soil is to miss the butterflies, the colors of pollination and the smell of their wings. Linear thinking works finely in linear systems, but nature is not a linear system, and her logic is love and lucidity, collaboration and care. She needs artists, not soil builders. But it is not science's fault or the cow or, perhaps, even the how. It is mine; it is yours. The dramatists are the fault of modern times and there, in the supreme humility and humdrummery of that place, we can also be the solution. Yes, that is what Fukuoka and Shakespeare were talking about. But their solvent to humanity's dilemma is not found in the creation of more mechanization, technology, or progress. It is not in the construction of better roofs. It is art we lack, not science; poems, not progress.

I believe that poems require humility, holism, and time to be created well. To write a poem is to first understand our role in the rhyme, not as the architect of the sublime but as the organizer of the line. Poetry and its poet also requires a sense of holism, meaning that special place of interdependence and intimacy, where diction and dictionaries are combined long before the words the poet may find. Lastly, to compose a poem requires the poet to have the time to do so. Poetry is the crop of leisure, a crop that is nurtured and never harvested, respected but never retained. Poems are temples and lush meadows, soliloquies into life's soul. Like autumn adorned and crowned meadows, they do more than simply exist, they speak just as the butterflies and the bees, and the birds and the waning summer grasshoppers speak of beauty and pain and the wildly artistic chaos necessary to nurture relationship. They are everything that is needed and today we have great need.

But poetry is also the commonplace cloaked in the semblance of the new; it is the black walnut that casts away its yesterday for the hope of a better tomorrow—not for itself but for ourselves, the being of all of us. And, if it is anything at all, poetry is the momentary melody of the grassland that gives way to autumn's wildflower wilderness. Poetry is the flowers, the birds, the migrating monarchs grazing on crownbeard's nectar, the trees, the time, the being of all. Yes, if agriculture is the production of food, then it is not agriculture that Fukuoka desires. Poetry has nothing to say about tractors and bushels and hanging weights. Poetry has nothing to say. Poetry is about nurturing nutrients for all and not the cultivation of crops for the one. Poetry is as holistic and equitable as it is intimate.

In the process of cultivation, we have missed, I believe, the nurturing of moments and have left many poems unwritten and unattended to. The agriculturalist desires the perennial grasslands, highly functioning systems that produce overweight cows. They manage for a world yet green in the autumn and they manage to miss the poetry entirely.

The poet and its dramatist, on the other hand, desires the seasonally-undulating succession of wildflower meadows—impermanence within permanence, emergence within resilience. They manage for a world that commutes on the wings of the starling, holding on tightly as their wondrous and wandering craft darts and shifts and bends to catch that current or to feed on that fly. You see, poetry is not the letting go of control; it is not the letting go of human desires. It is the holding on tightly to that which makes us human in the first place—the choice of love, the art of the dramatist.

The difference between the agriculturalist and the poet is the difference of definitions, really. The modern dictionary defines worth as "good or valuable" and "useful or important." But this is the beautiful thing about words, you know. They are as much under the user's control as they control the user. And so, we dive deeper. The ancient etymological root of worth is *weorþ*, an Old English word from the thirteenth-century, meaning "excellence or noble." The masters of moments, the poets, they who have time to sit, to ponder, to observe the simple complexity all around them. It is they who convey *heaven's graces* into eternity, who understands the soul of words. In fact, if you have ever read a poem, you will know as I know that a good poet appears to not understand the good or valuable or useful meaning of words at all, and rather, seems to place unworthy words in rhythms that make understanding less linguistic and more intimate and novel. Yes, poetry is the noble regeneration of the soul of words.

You see, there is nothing valuable in excellence or nobility outside of life's community. The poet without a corresponding society is not a bard but the butcher of literature. He is Mark Twain's Huckleberry Finn who "light[s] out for the Territory" to escape Aunt Sally's civilization—one who forsakes the citizenship of the commons for the hermitry of individualism.

But our flaxen-haired fairyland is waiting. The autumn blaze will not last. We left our boots inside and now walk barefoot, for furtive is the passing way. Gently we walk amongst the cacophony of colors, careful not to step on the many monarchs swaying in the windswept wildland. Life's beauty and purpose is often overwhelming. This is poetry, and we mourn for and hope in the regeneration of the poet. The nurturing of abundant landscapes is the co-creation of rain-soaked country, not through inputs but moments. Yes, regeneration and its agriculture is the nurturing of moments.

Oh, look! Whitman is also here, covered under this yellow duvet, a smile piercing through his aged and white beard. *Yes,* he whispers. *This is the origin of all poems,* of all things. This is stardust. Individual atoms dancing within the wildflower dance of autumn for the co-creation of beauty everlasting in the hearts of the poem itself—of the poets themselves. Regeneration needs poets; rain dances, yes, they need dancers.

The fairyland's autumnal blaze demonstrates the worth of the individual within a society. The society is the meadow, grounding as it is uplifting, but it is the individual beauty of the sunset, the oak, the walnut, the soil oozing upwards between our toes, the bursting crownbeard in our nose that co-creates the explosion of the senses, the nourishment of all, the resilience of a dark and clouded country.

TWELVE

The Learned Fool

We,

The novitiate of Nature,

The cadet of Creation, labor within

The fantasy of the fairyland.

We,

The all of us,

The only us, dance—and

The earth swells.

We,

The purveyors of the dust,

The catalysts of the carnage, perspire—and

She brings the rain.

Not brings—is

the rain.

We,

The dancing fools,

The wet and

Soaking and

Soggy fools,

        smile.

THIRTEEN

The Story of Oak

The crisp, warm evening of August descended loudly upon her desiccating surface. A mild and moist air worked its way westward across the yellowing landscape, a memory of spring, a rotund reticence. The east-born eddy echoed atop the oxidizing and dry summer grasses that were themselves waving not in its wind but in a dance of their own. A rain dance, perhaps. All had fallen into an energetic stillness that was patience, and time collected itself into a shimmer that, for a moment, suspended above us and then fell once again in silence.

The early autumn and discursive wind is a peripatetic pupation. It is the silent but essential middle ground between the bursting and youthful energies of summer's growth and the grey and harsh gales of winter's formality. It is life moving in reverse, and it is here that our story begins.

In the heart of the Wildland lives one of the oldest trees in our community. She is older than the land grants and she is stronger than the landlords, for she was granted lordship over this land in times immemorial. Not her exactly, for nature is never exact and this aged oak has many singing sisters that dot the landscape with ancient and harmonic rhythms. But in form, for even she knows that this land's lord is heaven-bound. She is a memorial that is a war-torn cenotaph of those fated oaks who sprouted but never grew, those who grew but never matured, and those who, when mature, were cut for your kitchen's cabinets. She is aged wisdom, which the venerate enthroned.

How do you plant a tree?

Wrong question.

What tree should we plant?

No. That is still the wrong question.

How do trees grow?

You are getting warmer.

Why do trees grow?

Yes, you found it.

Under the falling evening and upon its desiccating canvas, we worked the herd from here to there, as we often do when here's job is done and there's job is yet undone. We were busily attending to life, but this oak was busily attending to her death. It was as if she wanted her death to be witnessed, for she waited for the herd to move and she waited for us to look. How very kind.

Against the prevailing celestial coils, she splashed earthbound and ripped her rooted origins skyward. She fell uphill, upwind, and to the east and ignited a revolving evolution—a yin-yang of order and chaos and excess and balance simultaneously. It was a fair death and her "knell was knolled," to borrow from Shakespeare's *Macbeth.* Her death was infinity circling continuously within the limit of the canvas. But *splashed* is not the right word, for splashes require ripples and the succeeding stillness suspended in silence. Breaths were held, no one moved, and even the cows seemed to take notice of the vacuum. An empty clamor pushed back the silence that distended and then closed again elastically. For a long moment, life floated endlessly from here to there, and our hearts sunk deep in our bellies. Grief, regret, divine relief, and unutterable love saturated the scene, and all seemed to transmute into the firm freshness of a new weed that is supple. Life is sinuosity and death is the reminder. Why didn't we spend more time under her great boughs? Why didn't we care more? Why didn't we?

It is very human to interrupt the flow of life with purpose. When the oak falls, the great work begins—bucking and sawing and splitting and burning. Some even struggle to wait for it to fall at all and start the process early, like midnight shoppers for deals. Commodities may be finite but are oaks? The phylogenetic chain has much work to do.

Many centuries before this moment of death, our oak was born. This is her story.

Long ago, a Mother Oak's legacy extended into the heartwood of her daughter. Releasing her autumnal seed, she beckoned her friend the squirrel, knowing that a careful distance is needed for proper maturation and the forgetful squirrel is a fine distance runner. About a hundred yards from the outer reaches of the Mother Oak, in the open field where cover and shelter are sparse and the summer sun burns what little cover is left, the red-tailed hawk seized its opportunity. It was perched in the khaki-colored and autumn-stained upper limits of the Mother Oak, and it watched as our distance runner made its way. The squirrel stopped atop the mounded ridge for breath or break, and the hawk watched patiently. *Here, yes. A fine spot,* the squirrel said as it placed the acorn in the earth. *Here, yes. A fine spot,* the hawk screeched as its plunge stunned and its talons took the forgetful but obedient runner, its weight the moment made weightless.

Winter's winds brought rains, and the rains brought the deer to their wooded beds, and life hibernated. The landscape froze, and a clear mirror covered the earth, a hiemal harbor for the once-waving and dancing and singing grasses. The days dawned cold and grey, but the daughter was at work. Its concealed and hypogeal germination steadily progressed in the warmhearted womb of Mother Earth. Its embryonic cotyledons sprouted underground, the energy of photosynthesis—a gift of her Mother Oak, given as the placenta of the seed that matured in the earth's communal womb. In the darkness, light worked. The acorn feasted on the stored light of yesteryear, and in the springtime, she was born.

Emerging from their icy inertia, an oak's spring surge of showers is a symphony of colors. They first blanket their boughs with soft and down-covered and silvery-pink ornaments that reminds nature walkers and bird-talkers of her autumn decline. Their rebirth begins in memory. They then adorn their boughs with translucent and nearly-neon lenses of the heavens that gently settle with summer as cloudy and white-emerald wardrobes of wonder. Let us wandering few wonder together.

But the daughter's spring sprout displayed none of these oaken symphonies. While the vibrant and variegated vibrations of the Mother Oak often halt the axe, our sprouting acorn's success depended not on her grandeur but on her thrift and secrecy, for the spring animates the ungulates once again. And so, to protect her daughter, the Mother Oak beckoned for Grandmother Briar, knowing that an ungulate's distaste for the prickly unknown is greater than its taste for satiety. *I am here, my little oak,* Grandmother Briar whispered as her first thorns made themselves known in the red-brown coat of a white-tailed deer. *I knew your mother when she was your age, but that was a long time ago.*

Time passed as it tends to do, and our Daughter Oak grew straight through the heartwood of Grandmother Briar. Her upward reach remained unscarred by the passages of time and its webbed echelons of energy, for Grandmother Briar never left her side. Songs of the Spanish wafted north, and tales of a strange new life emigrated over the once-silent landscape, but our Daughter Oak cared not. Silence is an odd word to describe the pulsating and pounding dance of life that is already living loudly, but silence is what she knew well, and in silent patience, Grandmother Briar steadily worked.

The Daughter Oak steadily grew, and as she grew, her youthful canopy covered the landscape, providing shelter and shade on the mounded ridge. Hydrology hued the landscape green, and the squirrels once again returned, running and depositing food and seed, and the hare and the field mice followed. Jays and goldfinches awakened the skies, and the mockingbirds mocked and made mimicking melodies that healed the miasma of the once decadent and desertifying ridge. Life reawakened from the deep and steadily clothed the landscape in the bygone and bewitching colors of antiquity—yellows and oranges and yellow-orange hued homilies of subtle greens and snowy-whites and the black-eyed delight of the sun's figurines.

But with life comes death, and the hodgepodge of this marvelous mess places space and time as secondary to the purpose of the divine. *Transformation is amaranthine,* the Daughter Oak said to Grandmother Briar. *It is beauty and pain and chaos and change everlasting*. Her now mature and silvery-pink spring leaves transformed into the white-emerald and verdurous vestments of spring.

The daughter matured into the Mother Oak anew. *Thank you, my dear friend, you have been so kind to me. I will call you again when it is my time,* she said. But Grandmother Briar replied in silence, for her work well she knew, and her time well she had spent. In the silence of spring's last frost, she disappeared, the meadowed phantom.

Splash. Nearly four hundred years later and against the prevailing winds, our once daughter and now great Mother Oak tired, and her time-drained boughs fell back to the mounded ridge of her origin. In the darkness, light once worked and now, in the light, darkness consumed her. She lay like a spider over the landscape, her many and once-adorned arms now lay prostrate and naked and strewn this way and that. For half a millennium she worked upwards; today, she worked down.

While silent, her splash worked, and while working, her silence signaled new life. In the converging heart of two of her bough's union, where the undulating ungulates and the Wildland's cattle dare not to venture in fear of a tangled trap, life emerged—reemerged. *Hello, my dear Grandmother,* the darkness said. *You once protected me and now let me protect you.* Grandmother Briar returned, *Thank you, and welcome home. We've been waiting for you.*

In the darkness, light worked. The fallen oak sheltered the Grandmother Briar in the tangled heap of her fallen life, and soon our story will start over again. A new Daughter Oak will emerge through the heartwood of Grandmother Briar's loving and age-worn core once more.

Life is not the continuous adaptation and evolution of species. If it was, it would be about passivity and response and not activity and purpose. Rather, life is the active participation in the co-creation of relationship. The Mother Oak, the Grandmother Briar, they dance. This is the art of life, the choice to give and to be, to die and to give once more. Regeneration often focuses on oaks, but it is Grandmother Briar that is the dramatist, the great artist of abundance. She is the tree-tubes of our wonderful world and she is needed. Does your landscape's management allow for briars? That is your choice. She is waiting.

RELATIONSHIP IV

Of Singularity

Her influence encumbers not beauty but heaves the bend. A weightless wave, a lug of legs, a silent wager. She descends to pull life upwards and she descends to make the moment rise. The drought-downed and blanched boneset responds by stiffening its hollow core, its phloem, and its fervency becomes the frame. But our eyes converge just in time to catch her climb. She is once again on the move. Five breaths down and just two blinks to the left, she lands on her home that now rises to become her throne. The pontifical plantain replies by spreading its motley and ovate palms outward, releasing a heart of fleur-de-lis. It is the heraldry of the meadowland. Here, she lingers long enough for our eyes to see what they will never understand, and long enough for that which we will never understand to turn into that which we will never see, and she seems to stare at us through those dark and half-cut spheroids that are concomitantly curious and apathetic. The breathing and blinking bystander, we once again converge in the great meadow with her, the Great Being, and a delicacy made sure in the feathery force of her startling gravity saturates the scene. *Nature's laws are beautiful*, she says. Her voice vibrates the plantains' rivulets of reproduction. Or was that the wind? *But they are laws, did you see them?* Like a stubborn star, she then shoots upward, like pollen and plantain and the late-summer's boneset climbing, climbing, climbing up into the heavens once more—our eyes once again the chassis of her climb. Who is she?

From the roof of the world, language descended. Words join being with action, and they prove what is unseen as seen and receive their verification in its turn. It is in this way that words are also divine, both in the world of real things and the world of history. It is increasingly clear that the amelioration of any species follows the acceptance of its perspectives. To regenerate the forest, we first have to see the forest as a tree sees the forest—to the best of our human abilities, that is. We then must steadily work through the leaves and their waving communities, the mycelia and their networking exchanges, the ungulates and their undulant desires. In the same way, to well affect the world as a whole, one has to start with the individual perspective shared by the whole, that is, the divine.

How do we know what we know? Dreams and dreamlike ideas surround consciousness. It may be true that actions result from thoughts but are all thoughts conscious? Our normative condition is congruently conscious and subconscious simultaneously, and it is somewhere between these two unabridged states that the divine speaks its loudest. How do we know? How many times have you reacted to a threat, an incoming car that swerved at speed across the solid line for instance, with movement beyond expected ability? What you expect is what is conscious, that which is daily and clear, and moments made more clear by the light of the day—the road, the lines, the speed, the danger. What surpasses your expectation is what is subconscious, your quick and unexpectedly immediate dodge of the incoming mass of metal—of collisions, of death. *Whew, thank God,* we sigh somewhere between conscious and subconscious thought, and when delightful but heart-pounding relief hovers in the air. It settles as pins that stream down your spine and hit your pelvic floor only to rebound again up, up, up into consciousness. In the simplest terms, the divine lives in this middle ground, where what we expect meets what we do not expect but already knew could be true. The divine is what could be—that is, be above the miasma of the massed metal of this pin-pulsing and heart-pounding ground of thought and action.

The incumbents of life's co-creation, we participate daily within the conscious or subconscious belief that this all *could* be good. How do we know? We are let down when it is not good as if the "it" owed us something else. We are disappointed when good things happen to bad people as if people acting badly was a divergence from some expected order. And we are disheartened when bad things happen and heartened when good things happen. Are we not to trust our hearts?

While humankind by nature is not good, we eternally seek the good—maybe, our hearts seek the good—and we perceive those who are not seeking such as somehow less than human. How do we know? Do people remain good when unpoliced? Do they remain as people? *Homo homini lapus*—"man is a wolf to man." Yes, *Homo sapiens* universally across time have been wolves, from the Assyrians tearing off the conquered youth's testicles to then burn them alive as effective effigies against rebellion, to the modern Nazi's systematic extermination of an entire people because of their race and their beliefs.

The Nuremberg Trials stand as a fine canvas for our inspection. *Holokauston* from the Greek *holos,* meaning "whole" and *kaustos,* meaning "burnt," the mass slaughter and cooking of a race of people describes quite generally the word holocaust and quite strongly the idea that there is something transcendently true about good and evil, that certain actions stand above a society's relative individuality. Regardless of our knowledge, we disdain evil and feel that our relative individuality's disdain is universally true. How do we know?

Operation Reinhard was the Nazi's largest single murder campaign, where in three death camps—Belzec, Sobibor, and Treblinka—nearly two million Jews perished in gas chambers in just one hundred days. To put this in perspective, that is eight D-Day's worth of United States military deaths every day for one hundred days straight. The mass slaughter of Operation Reinhard comprised nearly twenty-five percent of the deaths in the Holocaust, while only occupying less than four percent of the timeline. Mangled and swelling human bodies stacked so high and so thick that even flies and their maggots became overwhelmed.

Odilo Lothar Ludwig Globocnik was one of the principal organizers of this human harvest. At the war's end, he shot himself in the head and rendered himself quickly and painlessly dead. This angers us, for his suicide feels less than sufficient and feels so entirely disappointing—a gentle and quick end to someone who brought millions of women and children to a screaming and painful and horrific and slow and simmering end. Unsatisfied, we want turbulence, turbulence that is also justice but turbulence regardless—turbulence against evil by our own hands and not his. How do we know that we are not good but seek the good? Globocnik, his blood-stained but now perfectly still and peaceful hands speak most deafeningly.

Beyond our heart's seeking of the good, we also occupy the time in which the good dwells or does not dwell. The idea that this is all one grand curiosity of coincidences and that we are all simply survival machines stands oddly in conflict with Darwin's ideological system of change over time. *In the beginning,* density and temperature combined and exploded, the effects of which we are still feeling today, the scientists tell us. This big bang is problematic in describing our origins though, as it could not have happened *in the beginning*—in the origin. The big bang was not an event that happened in time, for space and time and the matter in which time is felt and measured within space would have been created by its explosion. This, unfortunately for us, is a problematic word to describe an expression—a budding vocabulary, really—of an explosion and not an explosion of energy itself. Energy was created by the explosion, and, therefore, the expression of the explosion created the function of the explosion, and so we have arrived sufficiently in the words of Genesis and John, that is, *In the beginning was the word*, yes, and *it created.*

But scientists know this. They observe a universe that is expanding toward the infinite. The heavens are a cone they tell us, widening from the past through the present and into the future. Time is a member of this cone just as you and me and matter and the other stuff all around us are also members. As the cone separates toward the taper, the expanding matter and time and everything else cools and slows down, which also means that when it was all less separate it was less cool, and it did whatever these things like to do faster. That is, at some point in the past, the universe and its matter was hotter and more energetic than it is currently. As we retreat into this fiery past, our search for beginnings terminates when material particulates are so close to one another that they exist at no respective distance at all, and density, temperature, and the curvature of the universe become infinite. Scientists describe this as the state of singularity, the beginnings of the universe, when the singular created the many. Yes, but we already knew that—it is chaos.

But it is also the divine. The divine's normative and singular condition is Creative, and humankind's co-creative energies within this canvas are the unabridged stories between the conscious and subconscious joining of being with action. Increasing isolation is the dominant decree of the dunce-cap theory of the universe. Is it so strange that it is also the dominant decree of modern man? Increasing intimacy is the telling of a new story, a story that is actually quite old—it is literally from the beginning. This new and concomitantly old story is a solution to loneliness, irrespective of if science and its lonesome story believes it needs a solution at all.

Without community and intimacy, life becomes a matter of practicality, and that is practically worthless, even in a cosmos that is infinite and expanding into nothingness. In other words, what *could* be good is also what the divine already *is*—endless and ethereal intimacy, love and heat and community beyond knowledge, and time and space that is also very good.

This creationist framework of the divine and singularity is not the demystification of the natural world. No, that is where I think we get it wrong. Rather, it is the great mystification and animation of the world as a whole that places power in the all of us, the created us, and it is this power we seek when we seek the good.

During the Late Neolithic Period, the Proto-Indo-European language (PIE) emerged. It is believed to be one of the first written or at least first known to be written languages of the world. It predates the writing of the Hebrew book of Genesis in the same way that energy predates its exploding expression. Its word for Genesis is **ǵn̥néh$_3$ti*, a third person singular, which means quite literally, “to know.” It is constructed from **ǵneh3-,* which means “to recognize” and *-né-, which forms transitive imperfective verbs from perfective intransitive roots. Said another way, **ǵn̥néh$_3$ti* is the word for *recognizing* what we already *know* but, through that recognition, it is made more whole when it is known together. That is, when it becomes less lonely. Knowledge, to be good, cannot be lonely. This community-founded truth is the heart of the supposed big bang’s expression—which is actually just Creation, you see. *Bereshit* (בְּרֵאשִׁית) yes, here we are once again. Energy creates intimacy with density and time. To know something yourself is not the same thing as knowing something together, the latter making the former more full and somehow also more real—more good. The ancients are telling us that knowing is a community endeavor, but for it to be a good endeavor it must also be a divine venture—a cosmic struggle against loneliness, a terrestrial collision of the conscious and subconscious. The good requires holism, that is the unification of heaven and earth. Yes, that is *very* good.

The origin of our journey is **ǵn̥néh$_3$ti,* and it is also the end. It tells us that this is our story, but to be a good story, it needs more than our attention—it needs our dedication as well. That is, observation without action is worth little, and action without community founded in the divine singularity of all is worth even less.

To be clear, the divine in its simplest form is the manifestation of what Aristotle called *energeia,* or the "being-in-its-work." One who is wholly active in being wholly themselves, and this wholeness is wholly complete. Yes, the divine is holy and whole. But the divine is also ambidextrous—as the Creator, it stands outside of its creation, but as Creation, it stands within it—on and in the earth herself. The divine first creates, but it then imbues that which is created with life and purpose—and in the latter it enters this world as love itself. And so, what is the good? What is community? It is the divine, which is whole itself, made more whole when it also becomes more known—more in us and more around us and more through us. How do we know? We come from the beginning; we come from love.

Singularity is the fourth relationship of a dark cloud country. It is community at the core and subsidiarity at the source.

William Blackstone was an eighteenth-century poet turned legal scholar. His *Commentaries on the*

Laws of England is arguably the most influential treatise on law in the English language, and it provides an enigmatic teaching for regeneration. In his first volume, Blackstone lays out his *ratio*. As we consider action within community, the nurturing of the good—which is also the divine—we must contemplate his *ratio*: "the old law, the mischief, and the remedy." In other words, action within complex systems requires three things.

First, *observation through time*. That is, we must learn to see life through the eyes of those who are living it; we must see the forest through the eyes of trees and we must see through their sparkling blue-grey eyes via the mycelial lenses of yesteryear. It is to see the divine all around us. This is the old law.

Second, *acknowledgement through humility*. That is, we must monitor deviations from the good (the old law) by maintaining an open mind and heart. This can only be completed by humility and the continuous maintenance of our senses. To not care is the easiest thing one can do—to pass things by, to let things be, to forsake reality for the comfortable embrace of convenience, to let the next generation have it. Have what? Yes, that is the point. But regeneration is not about easy things, and it requires you to be uncomfortable, which begins with the humble acknowledgement that we have deviated from the old law, the good. This is the mischief.

Lastly, *advancement of the good*. That is, we must daily strive to reclaim intimacy and reawaken the energetic powers of singularity, of knowing, of the divine made more whole in the heated and dense embrace of community. This is the remedy.

To nurture the wild is to become a member of her community, and Blackstone's *ratio* lends operational commonality to the many and disparate experiences within this complex world through its uniform focus on the old law—the divine law—as the well-spring of everything else. There are a multiplicity of means that work to regenerate souls or their soils—if we just look at the grazing systems of herbivores, we have rotational grazing, management intensive grazing, adaptive grazing, adaptive multi-paddock grazing, total grazing, etc.—but, if Blackstone is saying anything at all, he is saying that both the means and their ends are of less importance than where they both begin and find their root—the why's. Yes, the virtue of observation.

Contained within this strange amalgamation of physics, English common law, and regenerative agriculture is the idea that the intent of the lawmaker is as important as the law itself. Said another way, the beginning of the universe somehow matters. The ancients knew this—from the Hopi to Hammurabi—and all had their accounts of beginnings, of creation, of the divine all around them. They tell us that the remedy is only as good as the observation and the willingness to act. The law is language with a bite, the persuasive energy of reason backed by the weight of influence.

It is a curious coincidence that the modern age of separation and solitude, made increasingly lonely under the large-scale simulacrum of sociality, is the same age that first "observed" a universe expanding and cooling into nothingness. Lost somewhere between here and there, between nothing and nothingness, these lonely thoughts are without the hope for either death or life. Dante speaks,

> Heaven chased them out, so as not to become less
> beautiful,
> And the depths of hell also rejected them,
> Lest the evil might find occasion to glory over them.

Our ancestors looked to the heavens and saw homes and heat and hearths and mysteries beyond time. But today we see a cooling wasteland that began on accident. Why are so we depressed? Why are we so lonely?

Singularity and its secret strength is the butterfly we met at the beginning. Do you remember her? That

Great Being whose influence encumbers not beauty but heaves the bend—a weightless weight? She is knowing made more known when she is named and loved and not just seen. Yes, hello, you, our Common Buckeye angel lifting, lifting, lifting high into the heavens. Yes, observation requires intimacy and names.

We are drawn to knowing because we are first known—we are the transitive imperfective verb that energetically emerges from the perfective intransitive root—the divine. Genesis—*ǵn̥néh$_3$ti, yes, we now know together. It develops and fixes individual sovereignty with meaning and purpose. This is the foundation of ancient and modern, pastoral and agricultural legal systems, and this is the foundation of regeneration. Actions matter, yes, but so also matters their primordial birth through humble and open and intimate observation. Then, community makes them buoyant. Perhaps observation is the wrong word, and it really should be self-inspection—*kavanah* (כַּוָּנָה) remember? For, what is observation but the inspection of the total self, the all of us, the created us. It is wholeness made more whole when a community, ignited with intimacy beyond time, simply turns around—they stop doing and start being. Observation requires silence—a silence understood as the singularity of the heavens. There in the naked and elemental and explosive reticence of reflection can regeneration plant its *good* root. Yes, regeneration requires reflection. Singular, its light emerges, and the universe warms under the nourished and *good* skies of a dark cloud country.

FOURTEEN

Grains of the Gods

The summer's intensity leaves with the chlorophyll, and the cooler temperatures bring the joys of calmer days. Chores begin to lessen, management transforms into planning and dreaming, the days early grow tired, the rain once again visits the parched landscape, and our souls begin to sink into the hearth. We spend our days watching wood burn and we spend our days thinking that this is just fine. Working as Nature may require everything you have but, in the autumn, she requires only patience. Under her cathedral of whispers made loose in the wind, we are transformed into the divine doldrum of waveless waters under a gentle wind. Patient, we wait until the first frost.

Patience is the prerequisite to foraging. To forage is to have faith—faith that nature, in all her busyness and occupation, has not forgotten about or neglected the ordinariness of humanity. Perhaps it is faith that Nature's patterns and cycles are as constant and rhythmic as they are inclusive and loyal. Perhaps even it is faith that Nature and humanity are just different words for the same thing, and the latter's ordinariness is just a different word for the former's often surprising sublimity. *Credo ut intelligam*—"we believe so that we understand;" we have faith so we may believe.

The autumn's welcoming chill shepherds a kingly and favorite forage in the Wildland. That is, the lush and opulent and wild American persimmon—*Diospyros virginiana*.

The best forage crops are great showmen, for their beauty and mystery capture the eye of the autumn sojourner and beckon the taste's curiosity and wonderment. The show begins in early autumn when the curtains of summer are pulled and stacked neatly back. *Diospyros* enters center stage shrouded in mystery. The lights dim and her shadow solidifies into an adumbration of age, the autumn equinox. Indirection her guise, *Diospyros* steadily works to conceal her gumball-sized fruits behind her dark and polished foliage. She is not yet ready; they are not yet ripe. In mid-autumn, her attempt to bolster the visual barricade intensifies, and her green veil transfigures into a red-hued mausoleum of summer and becomes the ornamental pride of the landscape. Our eyes are redirected to her foliage and not her food. Mystery yet reigns. But, with the frost, her green fruits ripen into a fiery red-orange, and her leaves enter their third act. *Diospyros*, the autumn pyros. Hers is a striptease epilogue conducted under the tawny-tinseled and fading limelight of autumn's final and enflamed moments. Yellowed, her leaves begin to fall, and her mystery begins to be known—her fruit is almost ready.

Upon exploring Virginia's interior, Captain John Smith wrote of the new and marvelous persimmon tree, whose fruit "is like a medlar," which is "first green, then yellow and red when it is ripe." But take heed, he writes, "if it be not ripe it will draw a man's mouth awire with much torment." Science in its wisdom claims that the frost's sting strikes the tart tannins from its fruits, making it increasingly palatable. But I like to think that, like myself, our tree is simply tired and needs a moment to rest. Like all in the autumn, she requires respite, a photosynthetic relief.

Diospyros comes from the Greek root *dios*, meaning "god," and *pyros*, meaning "grain" or "wheat." Translated literally, the wild American persimmon is the "grain of the gods." Grain in much of the ancient world was synonymous to life itself. It was the giver of sustenance, the driver of the economy, and the lifeblood of civilization. But grain requires cultivation and work and summer's distension, heat bodies made turgid. But the ancients murmur a secret truth whose harmonic resonance is hardly audible but just audible enough under the acoustic mass of modern machinery.

Many thousands of years before the *first* civilization of summer in the fifth millennium BCE and before the solidification of agriculture, the hunting and gathering and "non-civilized" ancients of Turkey erected the megalithic temple of Göbekli Tepe through geometric patterns of equilateral triangles that still stun archeologists and architects today. Did agriculture produce culture?

In Louisiana, Poverty Point stands as a supplemental and stark reminder of our observational faults. While the biblical Israelites were in captivity in Egypt, the pre-agricultural and hunter-gatherer Mississippian culture of North America constructed a sizeable and astronomically perfect, earthen complex that towered over nearly five thousand permanent residents. History calls them Poverty Point; they called themselves something else entirely—something else entirely more correct. Did culture produce agriculture?

The dominant narrative of the Enlightenment and its ensuring eras of colonization, manifest destiny, and complete ecological ascendency through force is humanity's story of progress from the state of nature to the curing state of civil society. From the seventeenth- and eighteenth-century writings of Thomas Hobbes to Jean-Jacque Rousseau to John Locke emerge the exceptionalism of civilization to quell the anarchic and addled archaism of ancient man. In his *Second Treatise on Government,* Locke argues that "in the beginning" all of "the world was America." America was the *tabula rasa*—the historical beginnings of man—and its seemingly boundless and primordial and "empty" land was, in a large sense, Locke's creation story. It was the political account of Genesis and civilization's opportunity for a second Eden. A landscape waiting for the colonizing and the enlightening force of civil society to awaken the primordial darkness on the face of its deep.

But the American persimmon knows better, and her patience prescribes a new and simultaneously old story altogether. *It is important to consider*, she says as her summer's breath gilded-autumn makes gold, *that your enlightened friends were not good lovers.* She shifts in her seat and drops a tawny and sallow-tined leaf, laughing as its drifts, drifts, drifts down to the earth. It is happy, for it is tomorrow's fruit. Smiling, the passing swallow lands on a lower branch, for it has heard this story before and wants a closer seat. *They were political philosophers,* she continues, *what did they know of my ancient origins?*

A westward gale picks up and lifts the fallen and jovial leaf once more and deposits it just beyond the reach of her canopy. A blue jay descends upon her upper boughs, her peripheral and soft wood waving under the windless weight. The jay's body is a perfect and pointed converging plane of the oriental sapphire sky and the frost-covered earthen podium that is talking about freedom. Were the ancients chained to our philosophy of progress? Was America an open Eden? Or were our ancient ancestors not also free to move and to do and to think and to be as they desired to be? Freedom is the singularity of the heavens made telluric when heat and density and time and the curvature of experience explodes expressively into the fiery origins of life itself—it is the chaotic art bound by the infinitude of celestial limits.

Patience and her search for freedom is what brings my family into the woods every autumn. We may spend the spring and summer nurturing the land, but today we look to the forest to fertilize our soul. On the first frost of autumn, you will find our family's hearth quiet, empty, and cold, for we are lost in the woods and are happily searching for our autumn grain—today, we walk with gods. Foraging for wild American persimmons in the Wildland's two-hundred-acre woods brings sustenance to our tired souls and lifeblood to our aching bodies. Husbandry is hard; love is harder, yes, but today we are foraging and need only patience. Patience is our guide and freedom is our force.

Elowyn, our oldest daughter who is five as I write this, is the best at finding the ripest and most succulent persimmon fruits. This should not surprise us, as only a child can truly see what nature illuminates. The taste of the fruit is equaled only by her joy in finding it. Sometimes we make a game of it and see who can fill a five-gallon bucket the fastest. Morgan, my wife, is good at this contest and often wins—such is the foraging power of motherhood. On occasion, we neither eat nor collect any fruit at all and find ourselves speechless at the feet of these ornate giants. Let us not forget that even *Diospyros virginiana* is not self-fertile and its fruiting potential depends on a partner, a lover, a community. *Singularity requires the community of everything,* she says. It requires a wholeness made more whole in the riming frost that observation freedom the forager made strong.

FIFTEEN

Awaken, Slumbering Heroes

The eradication of our soil,

the extinction of our soul.

That powerfully sacred thing

  that once made us whole.

Drought rises.

Sickness prevails.

Deserts widen.

And our climate is trying—

  to kick us out.

No, that is unfair.

We have long severed

  our relationship to the land.

          We have long since sensed

  the penalty of our choosing.

It is not her fault.

    It was our choice.

But choices are sacred things,
you know,
and their sacred realities
wield real power.
They are more than
simply terrestrial,
they are less than
overtly imperious—
Sacred Holism celebrates
the Created and
the Creator and
the Creation.

This impervious lens,
this sacred mythology—
a history endowed rhythm,
empowers
the dead,
the living,
and the still to be.

This choice is
powerful medicine.

SIXTEEN

A Liturgy of Lost Lilies

The level floor is deep in lady ferns, and Turk's-cap lilies dot the riverbank with remembrance. Their recurved sepals frame blood-orange petals that house earthbound and extruding stamens, which are hard to forget. They are bowing and burning, and their beauty often overwhelms. Echoes of bygone torrents reverberate against the waterway's channeled and eroding sides, its flow now placid in its bouldered bed. The small valley is formed by two sensuous and sinuous meanders in the stream, and debris is there locked in its way, creating a series of rotting dams that the beavers would have been proud of—are proud of. America's once-lost wetland restoration crews are steadily working their way up this tributary stream of the James River, and they are slowly making their mark.

In the upper river slopes, the snow-scorched leaves of Jacob's ladder steadily climb their pinnate staircase, gently working atop the brilliantly bashful blankets of gilded Trout lilies. They are the Turk's-cap's cousins, and their enigmatic community shelters the Wildland's time-endemic bluffs from erosion. No, not erosion—knowing. Clothed, ancient mysteries masked under modern manners.

Recent archeological excavations around this area have discovered what the wise among us already know and what the trout and their lilies challenge to show: these bluff headlands have been a home to Indigenous peoples for times longer than history has the ability to remember. Such are the powers and limitations of human inquisitiveness and its history, you know. We remember only that which we have the ability to know and know only that which we have the desire to see. The lilies and their ladders and their ladies have patiently watched our very human and heavy-handed happenings, and long have they kept silent. Why do *they* not speak? Why do *we* not listen?

The Wildland and this ridge and its river valley are the ancient home of the Siouan Indians of the Monacan and Mannahoac Nations. It is believed that just a couple steps south of this ridge and up its river valley is *Monahassanough*, a great city of the Monacans that was occupied as early as the Late Paleoindian to Early Archaic Period, or 10,000 to 8,000 years ago. It is important to note that the habitation of *Monahassanough* predates England's own geological and political identity as an island and island nation (England was a peninsula until 6,000 BCE when a great storm and tsunami eradicated its mainland cord). The ancients speak. Why do *we* not listen?

A white pine towers above the ridge, its roots extending deep into the bedrock, an anchor against the valley's blasting winds. Its wired branches are a feathered frenzy and a silent yet crazed chartreuse of chaos before the cobalt sky. A medicine and a muse, our white pine is also a lighthouse, for she signals and speaks. During the Paleoindian Period, rainfall in this river valley was about half of what it is today, and temperatures were ten to fifteen degrees Celsius colder. It was an arctic and coniferous-covered landscape of change—mastodons, wooly mammoths, camelids, ground sloths, and colossal carnivores like the short-faced bear were approaching extinction.

But so also was the forest. The climate was changing, and its community was evolving. *It is always changing*, the white pine murmurs.

The Early Archaic Period emerged on the face of this snow-white and pine-green deep like spring after a hard winter. The warming climate erupted waterways, and a strange spirit occupied our steam. It steadily cut its way through the rocky headlands to the level floor below. The Delphic denizens of the Dendron districts gave way to the deciduous decrees of the *duir*—the oaken forests of today. *Duir* is the Sanskrit word for "door," and these temperate giants emerged as the ingress to a new world—a warmer world. Over the countless years that followed, animals and plants worked with fire and rain and their winds, until waving meadows and wafting, woody canopies covered the landscape with relatives. Modernity calls them resources. Plants with palates co-created health both universal and particular.

Upstream, the spirit-scarred ridge forms a near sheer rock face against the valley. An algebraic symbol, a convergence of heaven and earth, when that which falls, falls not and that which sprawls, sprawls not. In the heart of this sacred union and its florid valley, our river runs and often forgets, as rivers have the tendency to do, about flow and the timelessness of rhythm and that undulating oak leaf, whose bronze-stained shimmer hooks the eye of that ungulate who is grazing the richness of the riverbank—a ghost silently passing in the morning mist from here to there and also to nowhere. Rivers are notorious conveyers of that which they do not own, and this is your standard river. The gravity subjugated rush of mountain water, the family-urged and upward surge of trout, the debris silently denting the depths, which finally finds a home when the beaver builds its dome. This is the river—it is everything because it is first and always nothing.

Next to the lilies and the ladders and the sound of spring mountain water and the drifting leaf caught for the moment in the beaver's barricade, an argillite point protruded, its dark and singular form an alien in the animated and sundry landscape. By using geochemical analysis at local universities, other points have been dated in the Wildland to the early Paleoindian Period, or twelve to thirteen thousand years ago.

It is not yours, the oaks whispered above my head as I picked up the tool and held it in my hands. The heliotrope-hued and two-inch-long point fell spiritedly through my fingers and plunged silently through the moss below my feet. *It is not even ours,* again whispered the oaks. *We are new here too.*

The wind tore through the valley and the waters appeared to recede like waves in the ocean, and a hummed hush echoed against its algebra, like a mother quieting her children.

Hush, she said.

Whose was it, the arrowhead point?

That is the wrong question, she said.

Who are you?

Maybe, I am Mokoš of the dawn-darkness or maybe I am nothing. But that sharpened stone is not mine either.

The lilies and the ladders laughed in their languages, but they are judicious, for they keep their grammar concealed in eternity.

The river then rushed rudely under spring's great weight, and the banks breached their bounds, and the lily-laden bluffs nodded their gilded grins to the earth in honor. The world darkened. Jacob's ladder climbed higher, higher, higher up the heights, and the ladies below waved them goodbye. Long have these emerald ladders witnessed the strident proceedings of humankind and long have they strode silently up their slopes. What does owning land have to do with settling it and what does industry have to do with ownership? It replies with only glacial silence and climbs higher, higher, higher.

Silence fell like exhaled breath, and its energy evacuated with it. The energy disappeared into the river valley's wildwoods to roam, to pursue, to be silently lost amongst the lilies and the ladders, to run with the great trickster, to be the river and the woods and that bronze-stained leaf now floating freely in the passage of time.

You see, regeneration, if we could use that terminology in such a pure moment as this, is the attempt to find this spirit, this silence. Not her in person, for I doubt she wants to be found—could be found. No, regeneration is the journey to find her spirit—that which emanates as the unseen energy but entirely perceived hush of the old-growth and oaken forest, covered and cloaked in the cathedral of the mother mycelia—that inaudible pounding of the meadows melodious and beating heart after a rainstorm, that succulence of spring after the last snow's melt, and the silent flutter of bees and butterflies and wafting webs detached in summer's gentle flush. Regeneration is the journey to find truth but not the finding of the truth, for that can only be revealed and never found—a gift. It is a journey, and it requires dropping your shears and opening your ears. It begins by taking off your shoes.

Regeneration, if it is about anything at all, is about me and you and the co-creation of a country so dark that its drought-stricken dirt transforms once again into rain-stained magnificence—soul and soil, the life of the all of us. It is the power of community living in mutuality, of the dance, of co-creating life itself, of clouds so dark, their weight, as though the moon, pulls life upwards. Yes, like lilies and ladders and rivers rising. And what rises, must fall. Will *you* fall with me?

You gave a damn! I am not surprised. We have work to do—let us together fiddle the night away.

Your friend, Daniel.

Acknowledgements *(and Smiles)*

When a book overtakes me, it often overwhelms my mind. For months, I cannot complete a sentence outside of my little library. Ask me what is for dinner, and I say chaos, or something silly like that. In this way, I owe a great debt of gratitude to my wife, who provided me space to write what I hear echoing all around me, and I especially thank her for deleting some of my best sentences. Words in their wonderful ways form phrases that are either melodious or aboveboard, but only the right words form the right phrases that make up the right sentences. If I can offer any advice this far in my life, I can offer what

Morgan has taught me: good sentences are worthless; the right sentences are a little bit better. I rarely find the right sentences, and my severe dyslexia makes sure that even when I do, they often exist beyond my reach, and Morgan makes sure you never witness many of my failings or fallings. What is love?

For the best people I know—my father for teaching me to urgently persist in patience; my mother for helping me understand the importance of the student's mind; my children for keeping me in joy and keeping my feet slow; my ancestors for giving me life; and Grandmother Oak who opened my eyes. It is impossible to write anything without the influence of community over my short years, and it is impossible to name all the happenings that contribute to my being here, and so, I will just say—thank you. Thank you to whoever you are and thank you to whoever you will become. One day, I hope we meet. That will be the *right* day. Until then, *shalom*.

ABOUT

DANIEL FIRTH GRIFFITH

Daniel is a storyteller, a hunter-husbandman, and a lover of the wildwoods. He is an undeserving father to three wonderful children and an unworthy husband to the best wife this world has to give.

A first-generation agrarian with a background in technology and entrepreneurship, Daniel's life pivoted after being diagnosed with a life-threatening and degenerative genetic disease. After seven painful years, he turned to farming as "the last resort." What he found was a life complete with abundance, joy, and health.

Daniel is the founder and director of the *Robinia Institute*, which in 2019 became the Mid-Atlantic Hub of the Savory Institute and today works closely with Allan and his team to advocate, educate, and demonstrate the abundance, joy, and regenerative power of holistically managed and wild living systems. Robinia offers holistic management and wildland ecology courses, apprenticeships, land transition consulting and system design services across the United States and leads the implementation of the Savory Institute's Ecological Outcome Verification (EOV) protocol in the Mid-Atlantic region. Under Daniel's leadership, Robinia is pioneering land transition and regenerative scaling capital and consulting projects alongside bioregion-wide producer network emergence to co-create a uniformly diverse abundance in their region.

Daniel also runs *Timshel Wildland* with his wife and three children, a pioneering rewilding project on their family's 400-acre emergent and process-led landscape in Central Virginia. Timshel nurtures peace, grass-fed and finished beef and lamb, raw goat milk and meats, happiness, and a multiplicity of wild and chaotic gardens that produce heritage poultry, heirloom vegetables, and fruits. Alongside pioneering systems, "The Wildland" in 2021 embarked on a journey, under Daniel's leadership, to develop a decentralized network of human-scale and ethical meat processing training abattoirs that utilize holistic field harvesting, whole-animal utilization, and a general lack of mechanized infrastructure as its foundation.

In October 2020, Daniel published *Boone: An Unfinished Portrait*, a wild biography of Daniel Boone that has, although not entirely highly-reviewed and received by the commons, become a pivotal work in the academic scholarship of one of America's foremost woodsmen.

In March 2021, Daniel published, *Wild Like Flowers: The Restoration of Relationship through Regeneration,* a book about regenerative agriculture gone wild. *Wild Like Flowers* within its first year of publication has sold many thousands of copies, enjoyed time as a #1 best seller on Amazon, was awarded an Indie Publishing Award in Nature and Environmental Essays, and effected the hearts and souls of the agrarian movement. The book received a wide array of influential reviews from Joel Salatin calling it the regenerative movements' "devotional," to Gabe Brown declaring that it provides the "words [that] so many in the Regenerative Movement are missing," to Judith D. Schwartz calling it a "buoyant riff that gets to the heart of regenerative farming," to Allan Savory calling Daniel the "poet laureate of holistic management."

Cover art by Sarah Griffith Howell

Sarah is a commission-based colorist landscape and portrait painter who studied under Masters such as John Ebersberger, Cedric and Joanette Egeli, John Clayton of the American impressionist tradition.

CPSIA information can be obtained
at www.ICGtesting.com
Printed in the USA
LVHW041327050323
740966LV00002B/16